THE GOLDEN DAY

Heaven always bears some proportion to earth.

EMERSON.

Lewis Mumford

THE GOLDEN DAY

A Study in American Literature and Culture

DOVER PUBLICATIONS, INC., NEW YORK

Published in Canada by General Publishing Company, Ltd., 30 Lesmill Road, Don Mills, Toronto, Ontario.
Published in the United Kingdom by Constable and Company, Ltd., 10 Orange Street, London WC 2.

This Dover edition, first published in 1968, is an unabridged republication, with minor corrections, of the third edition as published by Beacon Press in 1957. A prefatory note to the first edition, published by Boni & Liveright, Inc., in 1926, omitted from the 1957 edition, has been restored in the Dover edition.

Library of Congress Catalog Card Number: 68-17395

Manufactured in the United States of America
Dover Publications, Inc.
180 Varick Street
New York, N. Y. 10014

CONTENTS

Introduction to the
1957 Edition

The Golden Day Revisited

WHEN The Golden Day came out just thirty years ago, it had one distinction that the passage of time has now deprived it of: it heralded a new attitude toward our classic American literature; for it singled out and attached a special value to the period it named. To recall this is to emphasize what a vast change has taken place in the study of the American past, and in particular in the appraisal of American values and forms during the last generation. In time, the affirmative revisions started by The Golden Day were carried into the interpretation of the American contribution to architecture, painting, photography, landscape planning and urban design.

For those who are now immersed in "American Studies," the absence of anything like an appreciative attitude toward American literature and art before the present generation must seem almost incredible. But one need only scan earlier critical and historical texts in these fields up to the 1920's to see with how many misgivings some of our greatest works of art were still regarded—or with how few misgivings they were disregarded. At the time The Golden Day appeared, there were, so to say, no Vernon Parrington, no F. O. Matthiessen, no Constance Rourke, no Perry Miller, no Robert Spiller, no Makers and Finders Series, no full length studies of Emily Dickinson and William James, no five-foot bookshelf of Melville biographies, no fresh dissertations on Emerson, Whitman, Thoreau, Alcott, Poe, Longfellow, Hawthorne. Where today there is an overpopulated city of books there was then an almost virgin wilderness.

I set The Golden Day within this almost empty frame with
no wish to over-rate its importance: just the contrary, to explain why so modest a work could exercise the influence it actually did, from the moment when it drew such generous words
from George Santayana as might easily have taken away a
young writer's breath and his sense of proportion. That it did
have influence, there is considerable public testimony to show,
from the words of the late Professor Matthiessen on, to say
nothing of many more intimate confidences. During the late
twenties young people found themselves drawn back from
Europe, as their forbears might have in response to Emerson's
salute to Walt Whitman, because they suddenly realized that
"unto us a man is born." In this case, I hasten to add, the man
was not a person or a book, but a whole literature that had,
up to the nineteen twenties, never been unreservedly accepted,
even though individual contributions, Poe's, Cooper's, Longfellow's, Mark Twain's, to say nothing of Melville's and Whitman's, had become world famous. Until this moment, the
American spirit had been kept in seclusion, like an illegitimate
child, supposedly crippled, denied and half-starved by its parents, and rejected by the neighbors partly because of this very
denial.

The Golden Day did not, it goes without saying, bring about
this change. But just because it came at a propitious moment,
it pointed to the new attitude and for a while possibly symbol-
ized it. Before we Americans could recover what Mr. Van
Wyck Brooks had happily called a "usable past," it was necessary to have a fresh sense of confidence in our own creativity,
past, present, and potential; and this meant that we must accept
some better criterion for our performance than its approximation to standard European models. It was imperative that we
should, to begin with, cease our "ducking and deprecating" before foreign idols, and lift our heads, rather, to breathe the pure
morning winds of the spirit that had once blown over Grey-
lock and Walden and Cape Cod and fish-shape Paumanok.

Now this invigoration of our own natural hope and faith was
what actually happened during the period, roughly, of my own
adolescence, from 1912 to 1920. Who that was young then can

forget that stir of excitement, when he first read the poems of
Amy Lowell or John Gould Fletcher, Edwin Arlington Robin-
son or his younger peer, Robert Frost, or even, for that matter,
John G. Neihardt and Vachel Lindsay? Who can forget the
proud astonishment the young felt when Walter Lippmann's first
book, his Preface to Politics, appeared, or what fresh vistas
opened up with Randolph Bourne's essays and criticisms, so
firmly centered in our own country, yet exploring without embarrassment, indeed, with insatiable eagerness, as an equal
among equals, the rest of the world? Van Wyck Brooks' voice,
critical and admonitory, yet vibrantly confident, confirmed our
own sense of approaching maturity: no one could say so many
hard things about America as he then did who had not the im-
pelling faith needed to resume in his own right the role of the
"maker and finder." Though the first World War would
blacken and blight the more tender buds, those whose minds
were formed in the hopeful days before chaos dawned would,
for the rest of their lives, still carry order—a human cosmos—
in their hearts.

The novel, at this period, still lurched from the morass of
sentimentality into an almost equally maudlin swamp of realism; yet even there, if one cocked an ear, one could detect a
fresh note of high-spirited mastery: notably in an early book
that was, alas! to become the high water mark of the writer's
whole career. I refer to Ernest Poole's The Harbor, a minor
work that nevertheless took a special place in our imagination.
For a while even the dry words of John Dewey, justifying our
democracy by utilitarian and rational criteria, were, strange
though it may now seem, part of that general sense of libera-
tion: two leading critics of the new generation, Randolph
Bourne and Waldo Frank, wrote appreciative estimates of his
work. Before this, there had always been individual souls who
had gone their own way and found their own heaven, no matter how solitary the path or unfashionable the destination:
Hawthorne, Melville, Ryder, Eakins, Newman, Blakelock,
Peirce, Emily Dickinson, Henry James; outcasts, recluses, exiles,
leading lives of almost monastic devotion to their art. Indeed,
when one sees Walt Whitman in his proper setting, must one

not also put him, for all his bluff social manners, in this lonely group of "isolatoes," to use a telling word of Melville's? But now this alienation had ceased to be the destiny of the creative spirit: an army had gathered and was on the march.

For one decisive and altogether happy moment, these new forces, these new personalities, were mustered together in a new review, The Seven Arts: a venture whose importance for all that was to follow cannot be gauged in terms of mere circulation or length of days. And even when The Seven Arts passed out of existence in 1917, Poetry, founded in 1912, The New Republic, founded in 1914, and The Dial, revamped in 1918 then refounded as a monthly in 1919, brought to a fresh focus new perceptions about the nature of the American experiment and the importance of the poet and the artist and the thinker, as a counterbalance to the over-valuation of the pioneer, the industrialist, the business man, the engineer, the representatives of a civilization plainly threatened with barbarism from within, precisely because of this naive over-valuation. Weaving through all these efforts was a precious thread, we began to think, the thread of the "American idea"; though when, in due time, we faithfully traced that idea to its origins, we found it in Europe, and when we followed its consequences it became part of a much larger spiritual adventure than any complacent isolationist or "Know Nothing" could take in.

The movement these reviews began was to go on in various other guises during the twenties, notably in that joint work of H. L. Mencken and George Jean Nathan, The American Mercury; and perhaps I should not, out of modesty, neglect to mention The American Caravan, a yearbook that owed its existence largely to the passionate convictions and hospitable esthetic interests of Paul Rosenfeld, benevolently seconded by Alfred Kreymborg and myself. This awakening to the challenge of our own scene on the part of a widely scattered group of American writers and artists gave each of us the support needed for developing our own individual powers. Though few of us had perhaps read Emerson on Self-Reliance, it was in the spirit of that essay and of the American Scholar that we began to work. The days of our submissive tutelage in Europe were, for better and worse, over: this conviction formed the background for The Re-Discovery of America, to use the title of a book that Waldo Frank, one of the new leaders in letters, was to bestow on the movement, though for him a re-discovery in depth was even more important than the prospecting for surface ore easily carted away.

By 1925, at all events, the adolescent rebellion of the younger generation against our literary parents, and in particular against our aloof, ceremonious, seemingly solemn-faced grandparents, was over. Now that the break was definite and our independence established, it was possible for the young and the old to become friends, with delight and profit on both sides, as Frank Jewett Mather and Paul Elmer More were once so magnanimously to indicate to me. It was under these conditions that The Golden Day was conceived in 1925, and born in 1926.

Now, it would be a lapse of scholarship, to say nothing of a moral blemish, if I were to say that The Golden Day was the first book to usher in this grand revision of previous judgments and this instauration of the American past. The honor for that, even before Van Wyck Brooks' America's Coming of Age (1915) and Waldo Frank's Our America (1919), belongs to a work that antedated mine by almost half a generation: John Macy's The Spirit of American Literature. This book, published first in 1912, and long available in the Modern Library edition, has achieved a kind of modest immortality; and deservedly so. Before Macy wrote, the American tradition in literature was a strangely meager and erratic one: the popular framed reproduction of Our Poets, which so roused the indignation of Van Wyck Brooks, included Bryant, Longfellow, Whittier, Emerson, Holmes, and Lowell; but Whitman rowed no oar in that galley. When Barrett Wendell, who gave one of the first courses, perhaps the only university course, on American literature at the beginning of the twentieth century, published his History of American Literature, the balance of the text was poorly maintained and the tone of his judgment was often supercilious and even ill-bred. For him one sentence sufficed to cover all of Melville's work, and to damn him for "a career of literary promise which never came to fruition;" while he could find no better characterization of Crossing the Brooklyn Ferry than that it sounded "as if hexameters were trying to bubble through sewage." These judgments were provincial in the worst sense of the word, like the comment of the bookseller in Dorchester who explained why she didn't keep the novels of their Wessex genius, Thomas Hardy. "You may think well of him in London, sir, but down here we have a different opinion."

Certainly it was to Barrett Wendell's honor as a scholar that he at least recognized the existence, and even the importance, of American literature; and that he explored its products more thoroughly than anyone else had done before. But it was nothing short of scandalous that he should not have applied to a Whitman or a Melville a more universal standard, which had brought them recognition from England, France, and Germany; for by 1900 even Henry James, who had once been so callowly —and callously—condescending in his review of Drum Taps, loved to read Whitman aloud, and acknowledged to Edith Wharton that he was the only American worthy to be called our national poet.

John Macy's book was the first public rectification of a long series of provincial appraisals: singlehandedly, quietly but firmly, he established a new canon, which placed Whitman higher than Longfellow, Mark Twain higher than Harriet Beecher Stowe, and relegated to their position as minor writers people who had once been regarded as of major stature. So important was it to clear the forest of dead wood, so that one could get close enough to the big trees to climb them and measure them and gather their hoard of nuts, that there was a tendency, less in Macy than in those who followed him, to cut down some of the giants, too, especially if their immediate successors had crowned them with praise.

Macy's work was not flawless in judgment, for he left out Melville; but he escaped the later tendency to devaluate and debunk the great figures of our past: his omission of Melville was not a denigration but the revelation of a blind spot, singular in such a good Yankee as Macy, whose very forbears, notable among Nantucket whaling men, ought to have given him a family key to Moby-Dick. John Macy's revaluation gave place, in the twenties, to whole series of negative tributes to our classic writers; and in the case of shallower critics, professorial or popular, this attitude established a sort of inverse genteel tradition, which turned every sacred monument into a whited sepulchre. One of these humorless debunkers characterized a literary biography of the nineteen twenties as "the old-fashioned hero-worshipping sort of biography" because the biographer, after examining the subject's life with unsparing candor, still admired his work and respected his proud, battered spirit: the soul of Melville "standing alone, grim as a chimney when the house is gone."

It was no accident that the writer of that biographical study should have been myself, any more than it was that in writing The Golden Day I should have proceeded further with the revaluation that John Macy had begun. No accident because, before I had read Macy or Brooks or Frank, I had embraced our classic past with as much youthful fervor—and that was not a little—as I had embraced the new poets and philosophers I beheld, from a distance, in Greenwich Village, at the Liberal Club on Macdougal Street, or at the lecture-teas given by the Intercollegiate Socialist Society when Harry Laidler and Louise Adams Grout presided over its destinies. It was precisely my sense of the present promise that made the past so vividly alive to me: the past as I heard it come forth from Leaves of Grass, when I wandered with it in my knapsack over the Westchester Hills, or the past as I found it prophetically meshed in a future that had not yet dawned, in the Essays of Emerson, which I carried around in my middy blouse, in Cambridge, alternately with Plato, during the summer and fall of 1918, when I trained as a radio operator in the U. S. Navy.

Even before that I had, fortunately, read a large part of Cooper, all the Leather Stocking Tales and The Pilot and The Spy, again and again; I was eight or nine when, happily, I began buying reprints on coarse grey newsprint, with bad type, in a sort of cloth binding for only ten cents: a week's allowance. And before I was sixteen I had, of course, read most of Poe and Mark Twain, too; indeed, Longfellow, Whittier, Lowell, Washington Irving, Poe, and Hawthorne, though not Melville, had

been some part of our regular fare almost from the beginning
in school. (Strangely, I find that despite the wholesale revival
of interest in the American past, many of my present day students have often not made even a cursory sampling of these
authors.) In Whitman and Emerson I heard the voice of close
neighbors and friends; and by the time that Alfred Zimmern
invited me to give a course of lectures on American literature
at the new School for International Studies at Geneva, in the
summer of 1925, I was ready to tell the world about both the
old and the new. My qualifications for giving those lectures
were certainly not those of a specialized scholar: who, indeed,
apart from Carl Van Doren, William P. Trent, John Erskine
and Stuart Sherman, had even modest claims to be called scholars in this field at that time? But I had a qualification that was
at this point even more viable if not more valuable: I had
experienced American literature; it was an integral part of my
life, and indeed it had helped to shape that life quite as much
as any more concrete day-to-day experiences.

I must emphasize the nature of this preparation, for it explains whatever may be good in The Golden Day, even as it
points, just as generously, to what is lacking. Neither in getting
ready for these lectures nor for writing the book itself, a year
later, did I do a long bout of reading, conscientiously filling
in gaps in my knowledge. Though I made further notes, of
course, most of these notes were reflections on matters that I
had long been mulling over with no such direct end in view.
Instead of reading new books to complete my knowledge of the
author—at that time I had not, for example, read Pierre or
The Confidence Man or The Blithedale Romance or English
Traits—I re-read old ones, to refresh my judgment and deepen
my insight. As a result, nothing went into The Golden Day
that I had not lived with for a long time and had not fully assimilated. This explains my unreadiness, which even now I
do not regret, to pronounce judgment on my nearer contemporaries. What was involved was not the risk of being wrong,
but the bad taste of introducing a bright raw thread into a mel-
lowed tapestry, or mixing this year's wine with an old vintage.

The fact that I had first given the substance of The Golden

Day in a series of lectures at Geneva was responsible for one
of its distinctive features: its attempt to put our literature and
our national experience in a more general setting, that which
resulted from the breakdown of European culture and the split-
ting apart of interests and activities and goals that had once
been organically united. I still recall, with naughty pleasure,
the shock that my opening lecture gave my sophisticated European audience: particularly the effect of my polite demonstra-
tion that most of the qualities they loathed as "typically American" had had their origins in Europe. This was disarming the
opponent and turning his weapon against him with a vengeance. But the book was already in its first draft before I discovered how, through the mere weight and importance of the
work and personalities, I had concentrated on the period between 1830 and 1860.

That perception led me to change its original tentative title,
Running Streams, to The Golden Day. The first title carried
a suggestion of the old proverb, "running streams come clear."
This in turn implied that ideas that had been muddy trickles
at the beginning had, in the course of time, increased in volume and become clarified. But as I worked over the materials,
I came honestly to doubt whether the work my contemporaries
were creating, however excited I was by it, had anything like
the centrality and the depth that I found in the giants of the
Golden Day. So I abandoned the first title and even departed
from the chapter divisions in other parts of the book to emphasize the claim that I was making for this period, as in some
sense a source and an expression of our highest creativity: a
unique moment in the American mind.

During the early spring of 1926, when I was writing the first
draft of The Golden Day, Van Wyck Brooks was writing his
biography of Emerson. That book, when finally it was published, was to herald the change of attitude in himself which
made possible the Makers and Finders series. Brooks, through
his immersion in Emerson, had suddenly fallen in love with our
great literary ancestor and with this particular part of our past.
The elation of discovering that we were, independently, strik-
ing out from different directions over the same territory, and

were in our parallel movements well within sight of each other, gave a certain headiness to our correspondence during that period. Neither needed, at this point, to influence the other: we were simply held together in the same magnetic field.

In addition, certain changes in my own family life, above all our removal to a little hamlet in Dutchess County, where I was close neighbor to J. E. Spingarn, gave me a rural background not too dissimilar—and certainly not less rural—to that which Emerson and Thoreau had enjoyed. This included daily swims in Troutbeck Lake, much more of a pond than Walden Pond is, and rambles over hills and pastures more varied in contour and content than those around Concord. All this helped to give the book a kind of crystalline clarity, like the water from Troutbeck Spring, and from the mountain beyond, which of old used to be bottled and shipped to New York. As for Spingarn, he was a scholar and critic of rare quality: emancipated from pedantry by passion, imagination, and philosophic insight. Though I was never a disciple of Spingarn's in even faint resemblance to Thoreau's relation to Emerson, I enjoyed the stimulus of his challenging spirit: even his dark forebodings about the future, Melvillian in their grim unconditional willingness to face the truth, played a contrapuntal role to my own health and buoyancy, and gave me a firmer hold on reality: so that my debt to him, ultimately, in providing so much of the physical and the spiritual setting for The Golden Day, was no small one. Even when we differed most about ideas and doctrines, we loved, in ever deepening communion, the quiet glories of our landscape, including an ancient oak that had probably stood in the neighboring hill pasture since before the coming of the first settlers to America. My own life at this period, then, brought me close to Thoreau, Emerson, Melville, and Whitman; and if any fragrance still hovers over my Golden Day, who can say if it blows from Concord or from Amenia?

This concentration on one period of American experience and culture may well be questioned. Certainly it carries with it the perils of worshipping a dead self, and if it provoked an uncritical adulation, or if only the hallowed dead were celebrated, I might well share the misgivings that others have sometimes expressed. But there was nothing strange or peculiar in the fact that America had passed through such a formative period: we had but repeated the experience of Athens in the Fifth Century, England in Elizabethan times, and Germany during that *Aufklärung*, which was also its own *Erwachen*. Nor is there anything strange in the fact that such an influx of creativity comes but once, or that whatever further developments in art and thought may take place, they cannot have quite the pristine quality that characterizes such a moment, giving to all its works a kind of resonance that cannot be reproduced later by any mere exercise of skill.

Those who wrote the great works of the Golden Day could not, of course, be sure that they or their contemporaries had succeeded; nor could they, even when they lustily heralded the dawn that was reddening the skies, be sure that their own cock crow had helped to produce it. Does it not often need the passage of at least two generations to clear up the doubt that originality, by reason of its very departures, leaves behind? Thirty years is hardly enough to silence the condescension if not total indifference with which contemporary critics too often treat the most significant work of their time. For Lowell, Henry Thoreau was only a cantankerous eccentric, so ungentlemanly as to protest fiercely against Lowell's bowdlerization of a sentence in an Atlantic article of his. But given sufficient psychological distance, the classic quality of the great writers of the Golden Day, their originality, their daring, their high creativity, could finally be recognized. By 1926, happily, that distance had at last been achieved. The present, without facing about, could at last embrace the past.

For playing a part in that general recognition, The Golden Day could make a modest claim for itself, though the very nature of its leading idea was occasionally misunderstood or stubbornly rejected, even by those whose own views might seem closest to it. One critic characterized the book as a "crepuscular aubade," which may be translated as a "twilight serenade to dawn," and dismissed the dominant theme as a regressive exhibition of nostalgia. Nothing could in fact have been further from my intention, or from the mood in which I had written.

It was only because the great writers of the Golden Day were still so magnificently alive, only because their work was still so nourishing, indeed so life-bestowing, that for some of us who had been brought up in an increasingly arid mechanical civilization, committed to a pragmatic instrumentalism if not to a purposeless materialism, the youth and freshness of the Golden Day were like citrus fruits offered to a crew suffering from scurvy. To draw on that source of nourishment did not drag us back into an irrecoverable past: it rather made us fit to go about the work of our day, as Thoreau and Whitman had gone about their own.

Yet this singling out of our five greatest writers, in the very act of correcting old distortions and injustices, was not free, perhaps, from the sin of perpetuating these errors in reverse. In measuring the great peaks of American poetic achievement, I neglected even in passing to make an estimate of the foothills; and that fact, if it established their lonely eminence, decreased their apparent height, as Pike's Peak, from the distance, seems less imposing alone than Mount Rainier, with its circle of lesser mountains that give one a better clue to its height. The fact that this was a lapse of art seems to me even more grievous than the fact that it was a defect of scholarship; for The Golden Day was in no sense a factual survey of American literature, still less a close examination of individual works. Whatever merit it has comes from its interpretation and assessment of a literature already read and known. It assumes that the reader should have as full an acquaintance with the authors discussed as I had, and should be capable of correcting my judgments if I have erred, or of supplementing them if I have left anything important out of account. The emphasis is not on information but on evaluation: not on facts, but on forms and meanings: and in that sort of interpretation a significant sample may be more enlightening than the most exhaustive investigation. For me, a good book is a dialogue, and half of it is unwritten until the reader completes it. If that is true in general, it is pre-eminently true for such a book as The Golden Day.

All too plainly, the book has flaws; but I do not count as

one of the serious defects of this little study the fact that it concentrated on relationships and values, and sought to produce
a unified image out of a vast welter of details. This method,
one admits, did not become fashionable: quite the contrary,
in academic circles it was often dismissed as superficial, if not
somehow illicit, indeed, downright disreputable. Yet the need
in every generation for performing this kind of inclusive generalized critical revaluation should be plain, for the mere piling
up of details tends to obscure the design of the picture as
a whole, thus making the smallest and least important part
hold the eye so closely that one has no sense of the whole and
no sense at all of relative values. This was not proper work for
a specialist, but rather for one who, like myself, was dedicated
to the complementary role of generalist. Those who would say,
in response to this, "So much the worse for the whole" can
hardly be within shouting distance of The Golden Day, or, for
that matter, any other work of mine; and unless they wish to
lay themselves open to subversive doubts concerning their own
pious certitudes, I should not commend the book for their
perusal.

Even before the possibility of bringing out a new edition of
The Golden Day arose, I had occasion to go through the book
again, in preparing a course of lectures I offered from 1953 to
1956 at the University of Pennsylvania, under the auspices of
their American Studies group. This course, called American
Forms and Values, purported to go over much the same
ground I had covered in The Golden Day. It led me naturally
to ask myself what, in the light of fresh scholarship or my own
maturer judgment, I would change today. As concerns the special emphasis on the Golden Day itself I still found that I
would diminish or reduce nothing; but that I would rather
add and amplify, restoring for example a discarded fragment of
the central chapter that had included Alcott; indeed that,
even at the cost of blurring the original effect, I would enlarge
the book in almost every dimension.

The most considerable change I would now make is one that
I have taken the better part of a lifetime to formulate. This
has brought me to a fresh interpretation of both the romantic

and the mechanistic-utilitarian movements; for it seems to me that their coming together in North America created, for a brief period, a new kind of character, that which I have lately called New World man. (See The Transformations of Man: *World Perspectives Series:* 1956.) Under this interpretation I would regard the march of the pioneer as an attempt, following the breakdown of a unified Christian culture, to find a new way out from the repetitive impasses of "civilization" by making a fresh start on a more primitive basis. This effort, imposed by the very need to survive in the raw American wilderness, brought modern man face to face with the ancient realities of paleolithic and neolithic culture, on which the life of the indigenous Indians was based: in the New World modern man turned to the pre-civilized existence of the hunter, the trapper, the miner, the farmer, the fisherman and lived on this older level with a new intensity, as a conscious *release* from civilization—though fortified both with many civilized skills and with infiltrations of axial (Christian) morality.

Unfortunately for the ultimate success of this effort, the New World was opened with the aid of scientific and mechanical tools, from the navigation chart to the chronometer, from the rifle to the railroad; and in the pressure to conquer the wilderness and possess the continent with all possible speed, the mechanical side of New World man took precedence over the romantic side. So the new culture that the romantic writers, philosophers, painters and architects consciously aimed at, from Piero di Cosimo to Turner, from Rousseau to Emerson and Whitman, never had a chance to establish itself, though finally in the architecture of Frank Lloyd Wright the instinctual and the rational sides of New World man were symbolically united.

Properly interpreted, it now seems to me, the rise and fall of New World man is a more significant drama than anyone has yet portrayed, though the pioneer himself was doubtless only partly aware of the significance of his actions and the implied goal of his efforts. There are a few hints of this interpretation in my chapter on the pioneer; but if I had fully understood the significance of romanticism, I would have included this as a fundamental side of the American mind in the first chapter, even though the image of a new kind of personality did not come forth fully until the nineteenth century, in the character of an Audubon and a Thoreau, in whom an unstable synthesis of the romantic and utilitarian elements was actually effected.

But to put this concept of New World man in its proper literary setting, with sufficient substantiating evidence, would demand something more than the re-writing of a few chapters: it would alter the whole perspective of the book. Above all, it would give more poignance as well as more significance to the pioneer experience, for there was, in this muffing of a unique opportunity, an element of wanton tragedy. The hope of making a fresh start in this new land explains the constant note of rebellion that underlies our greatest literary expressions: rebellion against the political state, against the caste system, against property, against religious ceremony and ritualism, even, in Huckleberry Finn, against tidy routine and mechanical punctuality, as against every kind of cowed conformity. But in the very effort to escape the cumulative realities of the past, given in history and in memory, the pioneer chained himself to a present that had no concern for keeping alive the new values that he had experienced: so once he had conquered the wilderness he surrendered abjectly to the instruments that had made his conquest so swift—and his life so rootless. This whole aspect of American experience demands studious re-consideration; and if I ever attempted such a revision myself I could not confine myself to The Golden Day, but would have to write a new book.

Even apart from this, the original framework called for reconsideration. Almost as soon as the book was out I was prepared to recognize that I had failed to treat the period after the Civil War in the same positive fashion I had treated the Golden Day: I had rather made its writers symbolic scapegoats for the crass evils of their period. Despite its sordidness, venality, and corruption, this era had remarkably continued to nourish original artists in every department. If its public vices deplorably weakened those who, like Mark Twain, were still susceptible to them—*pace* the shade of Bernard De Voto!—it also tempered the metal of those capable of standing up to the age and dissociating themselves from it, like Ryder and Eakins in painting, Sullivan and Root in architecture, Emily Dickinson and Henry James in literature. In making mainly a negative presentation of this period I was following an unhappy precedent set by my older friend and mentor during the days of his own youthful dissidence. But Van Wyck Brooks himself was already purging himself of this error, in a profound change of spiritual polarity; and my failure to understand and sympathize with the writers of the post-Civil War era was all the more flagrant, since I was myself living in a similar period.

This negative and occasionally somewhat querulous mood is what, if I were re-writing the chapters on the pioneer and post-Civil War period, I would efface: not so much by deleting any particular passages as by surrounding my negative statements with more adequate appreciations.

That the creative minds of the Brown Decades were necessarily recluses, almost goes without saying: the cloister was a condition of their survival. Illness, testy recalcitrance, spiritual alienation were the price that they paid for their bare existence. Even if they raised their voices they could not be "heard" by their contemporaries; or, if occasionally heard, like Charles Peirce, they could not be understood. But note: the writers who seemed to remain most robustly in contact with their age, like Mark Twain and William Dean Howells, were perhaps in deeper retreat or more hopeless rebellion than those who, like Emily Dickinson, made themselves physically inaccessible. Mark Twain, instead of retiring from the raffish, money-ridden Gilded Age to save his soul, remained in it in order to pile the gilt on his own domestic life; and in the end that material gilt became the foundation—if I may pun about such a serious matter—of his spiritual guilt; for he ran away from his genius, and no man can look himself in the eye after doing that.

By denying his own responsibility for this act, Mark Twain earned, very properly, his own self-contempt; and to live at all, he had to transfer that contempt to an outside object, so that he projected it upon mankind at large. In What Is Man? Mark Twain said: "None but Gods have ever had a thought which did not come from the outside." This renunciation of their own latent divinity, this submission to external pressures in confirmation of a failure to develop that which lay within, betrayed those who were committed to success: but it did not betray an Albert Pinkham Ryder, nor yet a Henry James. Their survival during this period of the flashy and the sordid was a more remarkable feat, morally speaking, than the development of a Thoreau or an Alcott in the earlier New England community. So when all the facts are faced, the high quality of the best work of the Brown Decades is even more remarkable than the almost effortless originality and génialité of the period that preceded it. My failure to make more of this fact is one of the serious weaknesses, as I now see it, of The Golden Day.

This new assessment of the post-Civil War generation has, in turn, given me a better perspective on the work done by people who, with almost too-pointed emphasis, I had left out of The Golden Day: Whittier, Longfellow, Holmes. John Macy had taken a juster measure of these writers than I, in my high disdain of the obvious, was prepared to do. Happily time has scaled that particular cataract from my eye. How could I have been blind to the authentic indigenous note that is sounded in Holmes's entire series of Breakfast Table papers? Though this was plainly not the highest product of the New England mind, it still was a singularly original contribution. Did Holmes not make imperishable the homely urbanities of the oldtime American boarding house, that training school in psychological discrimination, with each individual the center of an unwritten novel: did he not, with his mixture of shrewd observation and worldly wisdom, create an image of our past as poignant and irrecoverable as that of the clipper ship and the covered wagon? True, the dapper little doctor could not appreciate Whitman and he was all too eagerly appreciative of the lesser products of his own wit, but that does not take away a whiff from the delectable odor of those Breakfast Table colloquies. That the Golden Day produced Oliver Wendell Holmes is in itself an important sidelight on the period.

Over my utter neglect of Longfellow, too, I would now smilingly do penance. In my reaction against my original dispar-

agement I am disposed, perhaps, to be more appreciative than
Macy was, even of those poems that made his popular place so
assured. The fact that they were popular is a proof, better
than the American free school or the free library, that the political democracy of the founding fathers had been able, in two
short generations, to conquer the world of letters and achieve,
if only at a low level, a universality that embraced other peoples. Walt Whitman saw the significance of Longfellow in that
light; and it was snobbish presumption, if not worse, for a later
critic to misread the lesson of Longfellow's popularity.

Admittedly, many of Longfellow's most famous poems have
little to commend them esthetically. But the person who can
say this of the opening lines of Evangeline, and of remarkably
sustained passages scattered through that long poem, has no ear
for their Homeric gravity, nor has he sufficient perception of
the effect of the long ocean roll of those hexameters in making
possible the great rhythms of Out of the Cradle Endlessly
Rocking. In the case of Hiawatha, one must acknowledge that
Longfellow's effort to use our native materials, treating the Indian as an active member of the spiritual community, could
not satisfy either the literary taste or the anthropological
knowledge of a later generation. But such experiments are not
worthless even when they are failures: what Longfellow was
thus saying and doing was, morally speaking, important to say
and do. It was better to "play Indian," as children used to do
before they aspired to the more primitive role of "space-men,"
than to shut one's mind and heart to all that we, the non-
indigenous intruders, could learn from the primitive lords of
this land. Here, as in Longfellow's early response to the cause
of abolition, his moral sensitiveness was exemplary; and it
partly offsets his tepid esthetic expression. It was our own failure as a people to follow the lead given by Cooper and Longfellow, in their appreciation of that great primitive heritage
which we might have helped to keep alive, to our own benefit
as well as that of the people we so wantonly neglected and despised—it was this, and not Longfellow's failures of realism
that we should be critically aware of. Our Mary Austins and
Paul Radins came all-too-late.

As for Longfellow's sonnets on Chaucer, Dante, Milton, they are worthy of the great poets they celebrate; and they go along with a handful of other poems that show him, if not a major poet, to be capable on occasion of writing haunting and beautiful verse. One grants, in the end, that he spent most of his poetic life mid the polite felicities of his comfortable living rooms; the very hospitality of these rooms, and the easy accessibility of his ample attic, filled with old trinkets, keepsakes, costumes, souvenirs of European travels, diverted him from the great wine cellar beneath, where the poet's true sustenance is kept under lock and key. But when Longfellow did, now and again, descend to that dark cellar, and stumble over its treacherous floor, he brought back bottles of incomparable vintage: witness the poem, unpublished during his lifetime, to his dead wife, she whom he had seen go up in flames before his eyes. That a popular poet could be so good in his high moments was surely more important than that a mediocre poet could be so popular: yet both were true.

But Longfellow has other claims to our respect, as I would now interpret the development of the American mind. The first necessity of our spiritual growth was a breaking away from Europe: more especially, a weaning from the maternal teats of England. That necessity Longfellow himself quickly discerned and proclaimed, from the moment he delivered his Commencement Address at Bowdoin on Our Native Literature. In that examination of our situation he pointed out the absurdity of writing about nightingales in a country that harbored no such birds, or of falling back on foreign scenes and foreign experiences when we had our own to mind and master. It is, indeed, hardly an exaggeration to call that address the salutary opening, with special reference to literature, of Emerson's The American Scholar, as Melville's essay on Hawthorne and his Mosses and Whitman's Democratic Vistas, are the peroration.

Up to a point the poet whose first published poem was The Battle of Lovell's Pond, the poet who allied himself to the despised abolitionists shortly after Whittier and well before Emerson, who sought out the Indian, the early settler, the revolutionary patriot, the homely trades, for his themes, lived up to his own requirements—as well as Whitman's—for an American literature rooted in native ground. Here Longfellow, with Cooper, was the leader almost half a generation before Leaves of Grass, Moby-Dick, and The Scarlet Letter were conceived. But Longfellow not merely sought to be fully at home in his own American world. He realized here, well before Henry James or Henry Adams did, how meager and provincial that world was: how much the American had lost, if not by committing parricide, then by running away from home; and how useful his abandoned inheritance would be at his coming of age, so that he might start, with fuller equipment, on his own career. So, partly as a poet, but even more as a scholar, Longfellow performed an indispensable function: he restored to the American the riches that he had renounced, and the family estate he had vowed never to visit again. Once the American had cut his childhood tie to the Old World, it became necessary for the American writer to reinstate himself in that world once more, as Henry James and T. S. Eliot did: as an adult and an equal.

Admittedly, more colonial minds, servile or timid, who clung to the Old World, could get no benefit from Old World culture: the poetasters and connoisseurs who returned to Europe merely to raid its markets and old curiosity shops, and to store up, in a private museum, the loot they had brought back, were incapable of creative activity. My most astringent words about The Pillage of the Past still hold; for in fact, as Henry James himself pictured these people, in that decadent American, Gilbert Osmond, in the Portrait of a Lady, their very taste and esthetic sensibilities had somehow become poisonous, and degraded their morals as well. So what I have said of Longfellow indicates in some degree what I would say, both in extenuation and in praise, of Henry James. What Longfellow sought to do, from Outre Mer to his translation of The Divine Comedy, became, in the stories and novels of Henry James, a source of potent creativity. There are moments when James's concern with the non-provincial breadth of Europe was itself a provinciality: his almost morbid concern for the refinements of craftsmanship, kept him from appreciating the esthetic power as well as the human depth of Tolstoi; but in the end, it did not blind him to Whitman or Browning, as a more priggish Europeanism blinded Santayana. James's absorption in Europe, so far from being a defection or even a defeat, as Van Wyck Brooks often seems to suggest, was rather a necessary stage in our common development. What seem to me both esthetically and psychologically his maturest novels, What Maisie Knew and The Turn of the Screw, lose nothing by this absorption. If Hawthorne was an esthetician of sin, James was an esthetician of corruption; in fact, he turned the base common metal of the Gilded Age into gold. No one, not Henry Adams nor even Marcel Proust, gave a more detached report of the dissolution of the European spirit than James did; nor did anyone else, for that matter, give a more timely intimation of the dreadful shape of things to come. How prophetic, how universal an application, in the light of all that has happened since, seems James's perceptive juxtaposition in The American Scene of "the family and the infernal machine."

This general widening of the horizon after the Civil War went hand in hand with an intense absorption in the local and the regional. Here I particularly feel in The Golden Day the limitations of my early reading; for this impoverished my interpretation of one element in American literature, the regional, where my own quick interest in geographic and cultural regionalism should have enabled me to make a positive contribution. Though much post-Civil War regionalism was born of a nostalgia for past times and past ways, then being undermined by the forces of mechanical progress, it was also an effort at self-identification and individuation and self-actualization in which other parts of our land followed the early lead of New England. Perhaps the surest way to "place" Mark Twain, and to center on the best he had to offer, is to regard him as emphatically a regional writer, never in his element, never capable of conveying his total sense of human existence, except in handling life along the Mississippi or in the even rougher Far West. In the local color writers the body and form of the country, region by region, at last became visible. New England, as usual, had led the way: for Hawthorne was the first to exploit these potentialities. With patience, attentiveness, reflectiveness, loyalty to something more than surface color and accent, durable works of art

might have been achieved. But how easily these writers were
drawn away: how quickly Mark Twain disobeyed his own precept, that one must write out of one's experience—he with his
sentimentalized Joan of Arc and his Prince and Pauper, to say
nothing of his Connecticut Yankee extravaganza, the most justifiable of his departures.

But in his proper role, Mark Twain was spiritually elder
brother to Joel Chandler Harris, to Edward Eggleston, to Hamlin Garland, and to a group of New England women, Sarah
Orne Jewett, Mary Wilkins Freeman, Louisa Alcott. The
work that these people did was permanently valuable, though
their technique—as in their stultifying pride in accurate dialect
—might over-reach itself. The immense variety of our regional
backgrounds, their very odor and savor, finally came through:
without their listening ears, neither Carl Sandburg nor Robert
Frost might so surely have been possible. The failure of these
regional writers to establish a firm tradition, their too facile se-
duction by American success, itself poses an interesting problem.
Whether the immediate loss of regional color can belatedly be
restored by any activity of the intelligence, stemming from our
regional universities, remains to be seen. In The Golden Day I
should at least have set the problem more clearly, instead of
gliding over it.

As for other revaluations, to make them adequately I should
have to do what I have firmly decided not to do: re-write the
whole book, and in particular to re-vamp my treatment of
Edgar Allan Poe, Herman Melville, and William James, as well
as bring forward Emily Dickinson. Yet I cannot withhold a word
in reparation to Henry Adams; for his was a mind whose greatness smothers his moral blemishes—his arrogant humility, his
cold superiority, even his ugly little streaks of anti-semitism.
When one has said the worst about Adams, one must still admit
that he, and he alone, had both the intelligence and the depth
of intuition to see something that was invisible to most of his
contemporaries: the disintegration of Western Civilization.
What is more, he put his diagnostic finger on the very spots in
politics, technics, and science, where the cancerous growth had
begun to develop. Long before the scientists concerned were suf-

ficiently roused from their sleep-walking routines to realize what they were in fact doing, Adams desperately tried to draw their attention to the more general transformations of society their discoveries were ushering in. He saw, if they did not, that the train of events set in motion by the accidental discovery of the Becquerel rays would, in time, threaten the structure of civilization, making "morality become police" and creating bombs of "cosmic violence."

At the time I wrote The Golden Day, I was more conscious of the sociological imperfection of Adams's historic scaffolding than I was of the sound structure for which, willy-nilly, he had laid the foundations. In other words, I then shared the smiling blindness of my contemporaries; and almost all that I said about Adams was not so much unjust as damnably irrelevant. Today, my contemporaries for the most part still remain indifferent both to Adams's warning and to the meaning of the present crisis in world civilization. If only because, being now awake, I can sympathize more fully with Adams's frustrations, I wish I had in anticipation done something like justice to Adams's most neglected side: the clairvoyance, as well as the scholarly historic insight, of his foreboding mind. Those who still condescend to Adams, as to a petulant amateur in science and medieval history, do not have the faintest insight into the world they are now living in. Their blindness to Adams's extrapolations derives from a more primal darkness: "invincible ignorance."

Such would be some of the emendations and additions to The Golden Day I might, thirty years later, have made. But each phase of life has its own values and its own claims. I still can remember my intense resentment, as a child, when a competent old uncle, in all kindliness, would correct one of my youthful drawings with a sure touch that erased my own blurred lines. The "improvements" seemed to me wanton and wooden, even if I envied the skill they showed. Since the lines of The Golden Day are still sharp and clear, I fear that any sophisticated later touches of mine would only, in reverse, blur the whole effect, and make the book esthetically as well as historically worthless. In all decency, I would spare the young man who wrote The Golden Day that agony, and that well-justified resentment on finding his work defaced. If The Golden Day is to remain alive, it will not be through a belated blood transfusion from my present self. For this reason, I have not changed a single sentence of the text. In a shifting world it is something at least to keep one's identity: that virtue this new edition still possesses.

LEWIS MUMFORD

Amenia, New York
May 1956—January 1957

Prefatory Note to the
Original Edition

THIS book rounds out the study of American life begun in Sticks and Stones. Where in the first book I used architecture as an index of our civilization, in The Golden Day I have treated imaginative literature and philosophy as a key to our culture. Civilization and culture, the material fact and the spiritual form, are not exclusive terms; for one is never found without at least a vestige of the other: and I need not, I trust, apologize because here and there the themes of the two books interpenetrate.

The substance of this book was delivered in a series of lectures on The Development of American Culture before a group of European and American students at Geneva, in August, 1925. These lectures were given at the invitation of the Geneva Federation; and I gratefully record my debt to Mr. and Mrs. Alfred Zimmern for their constant understanding and sympathy. Without the numerous explorations Mr. Van Wyck Brooks has made, it would have been impossible to make the connected study I have here attempted; and without Mr. J. E. Spingarn's criticism of the final draft of the manuscript more than one page would have been the poorer. The first chapter appeared in *The American Mercury*.

LEWIS MUMFORD

1926

THE GOLDEN DAY

Chapter One   The Origins of
the American Mind

THE settlement of America had its origins in the unsettlement of Europe. America came into existence when the European was already so distant in mind from the ancient ideas and ways of his birthplace, that the whole span of the Atlantic did not materially widen the gulf. The dissociation, the displacement, and finally, the disintegration of European culture became most apparent in the New World: but the process itself began in Europe, and the interests that eventually dominated the American scene all had their origin in the Old World.

The Protestant, the inventor, the politician, the explorer, the restless delocalized man—all these types appeared in Europe before they rallied together to form the composite American. If we can understand the forces that produced them, we shall fathom the origins of the American mind. The settlement of the Atlantic seaboard was the culmination of one process, the breakup of medieval culture, and the beginning of another. If the disintegration went farthest in America, the processes of renewal have, at intervals, been most active in the new country; and it is for the beginnings of a genuine culture, rather than for its relentless exploitation of materials, that the American adventure has been significant. To mark the points at which the culture of the Old World broke down, and to discover in what places a new one has arisen are the two poles of this study. Something of value disappeared with the colonization of America. Why did it disappear? Something of value was created. How did that come about? If I do not fully answer these questions, I purpose, at least, to put them a little more sharply, by tracing them to their historic beginnings, and by putting them in their social context.

II

In the Thirteenth Century the European heritage of medieval culture was still intact. By the end of the Seventeenth it had become only a heap of fragments, and men showed, in their actions if not by their professions, that it no longer had a hold over their minds. What had happened?

If one tries to sum up the world as it appeared to the contemporaries of Thomas Aquinas or Dante one is conscious of two main facts. The physical earth was bounded by a narrow strip of seas: it was limited: while above and beyond it stretched the golden canopy of heaven, infinite in all its invitations and promises. The medieval culture lived in the dream of eternity: within that dream, the visible world of cities and castles and caravans was little more than the forestage on which the prologue was spoken. The drama itself did not properly open until the curtains of Death rang down, to destroy the illusion of life and to introduce the main scene of the drama, in heaven itself. During the Middle Ages the visible world was definite and secure. The occupations of men were defined, their degree of excellence described, and their privileges and duties, though not without struggle, were set down. Over the daily life lay a whole tissue of meanings, derived from the Christian belief in eternity: the notion that existence was not a biological activity but a period of moral probation, the notion of an intermediate hierarchy of human beings that connected the lowest sinner with the august Ruler of Heaven, the idea that life was significant only on condition that it was prolonged, in beatitude or in despair, into the next world. The beliefs and symbols of the Christian Church had guided men, and partly modified their activities, for roughly a thousand years. Then, one by one, they began to crack; one by one they ceased to be "real" or interesting; and gradually the dream that held them all together started to dissolve. When the process ceased, the united order of Christendom had become an array of independent and sovereign States, and the Church itself had divided up into a host of repellent sects.

At what point did medieval culture begin to break down? The current answer to this, "With the Renaissance," is merely an evasion. When did it finally cease to exist? The answer is that a good part of it is still operative and has mingled with the customs and ideas that have succeeded it. But one can, perhaps, give an arbitrary beginning and an arbitrary end to the whole process. One may say that the first hint of change came in the Thirteenth Century, with the ringing of the bells, and that medieval culture ceased to dominate and direct the European community when it turned its back upon contemporary experience and failed at last to absorb the meanings of that experience, or to modify its nature. The Church's inability to control usury; her failure to reckon in time with the Protestant criticism of her internal administration; the unreadiness of the scholastics to adapt their methods to the new interests and criteria of science; the failure to prevent the absorption of the free cities, the feudal estates, and the monasteries by the central government—these are some of the stigmata of the decline. It is impossible to give a date to all of them; but it is pretty clear that by the end of the Seventeenth Century one or another had come to pass in every part of Europe. In countries like England, which were therefore "advanced," all of them had come to pass.

It is fairly easy to follow the general succession of events. First, the bells tolled, and the idea of time, or rather, temporality, resumed its hold over men's minds. All over Europe, beginning in the Thirteenth Century, the townsman erected campaniles and belfries, to record the passing hour. Immersed in traffic or handicraft, proud of his city or his guild, the citizen began to forget his awful fate in eternity; instead, he noted the succession of the minutes, and planned to make what he could of them. It was an innocent enjoyment, this regular tolling of the hour, but it had important consequences. Ingenious workmen in Italy and Southern Germany invented clocks, rigorous mechanical clocks: they adapted the principle of the woodman's lathe and applied it to metal. Here was the beginning of the exact arts. The craftsman began by measuring time; presently he could measure millimeters, too, and with the knowledge and technique introduced by the clockmaker, he was ready to make the telescope, the microscope, the theodolite—all of them instruments of a new order of spatial exploration and measurement.

The interests in time and space advanced side by side. In the Fifteenth Century the mapmakers devised new means of measuring and charting the earth's surface, and scarcely a generation before Columbus's voyages they began to cover their maps with imaginary lines of latitude and longitude. As soon as the mariner could calculate his position in time and space, the whole ocean was open to him; and henceforward even ordinary men, without the special skill and courage of a Marco Polo or a Leif Ericsson, could travel to distant lands. So time and space took possession of the European's mind. Why dream of heaven or eternity, while the world was still so wide, and each new tract that was opened up promised, if not riches, novelty, and if not novelty, well, a new place to breathe in? So the bells tolled, and the ships set sail. Secure in his newly acquired knowledge, the European traveled outward in space, and, losing that sense of the immediate present which went with his old belief in eternity, he traveled backward and forward in time. An interest in archæology and in utopias characterized the Renaissance. They provided images of purely earthly realizations in past and future: ancient Syracuse and The City of the Sun were equally credible.

The fall of Constantinople and the diffusion of Greek literature had not, perhaps, such a formative influence on this change as the historian once thought. But they accompanied it, and the image of historic Greece and Rome gave the mind a temporary dwelling-place. Plainly, the knowledge which once held it so firmly, the convictions that the good Christian once bought so cheaply and cheerfully, no longer sufficed: if they were not altogether thrown aside, the humanists began, with the aid of classic literature, to fill up the spaces they had left open. The European turned aside from his traditional cathedrals and began to build according to Vitruvius. He took a pagan interest in the human body, too, and Leonardo's St. John was so lost to Christianity that he became Bacchus without changing a feature. The Virgin herself lost her old sanctity. Presto! the Child disappeared, the responsibilities of motherhood were gone, and she was now Venus. What had St. Thomas Aquinas to say about theology? One could read the Phædo. What had Aristotle to say about natural history? Leonardo, unaided, discovered fossils in the Tuscan hills and inferred that the ocean was once there. Simple peasants might cling to the Virgin, ask for the intercession of the saints, and kneel before the cross; but these images and ideas had lost their hold upon the more acute minds of Europe. They had broken, these intellectual adventurers, outside the tight little world of Here and Eternity: they were interested in Yonder and Yesterday; and since eternity was a long way off and we'll "be damnably moldy a hundred years hence," they accepted tomorrow as a substitute.

There were some who found it hard to shake off the medieval dream in its entirety; so they retained the dream and abandoned all the gracious practices that enthroned it in the daily life. As Protestants, they rejected the outcome of historic Christianity, but not its inception. They believed in the Eucharist, but they did not enjoy paintings of the Last Supper. They believed in the Virgin Mary, but they were not softened by the humanity of Her motherhood. They read, voraciously, the literature of the Ancient Jews, and the legends of that sect which grew up by the shores of Galilee, but, using their private judgment and taking the bare words as the sum and substance of their religion, they forgot the interpretations from the early Fathers to St. Thomas which refined that literature and melted it into a comprehensible whole. When the Protestant renounced justification by works, he included under works all the arts which had flourished in the medieval church and created an independent realm of beauty and magnificence. What remained of the faith was perhaps intensified during the first few generations of the Protestant espousal—one cannot doubt the original intensity and vitality of the protest—but alas! so little remained!

In the bareness of the Protestant cathedral of Geneva one has the beginnings of that hard barracks architecture which formed the stone-tenements of Seventeenth Century Edinburgh, set a pattern for the austere meeting-houses of New England, and finally deteriorated into the miserable shanties that line Main Street. The meagerness of the Protestant ritual began that general starvation of the spirit which finally breaks out, after long repression, in the absurd jamborees of Odd Fellows, Elks,

Woodmen, and kindred fraternities. In short, all that was once
made manifest in a Chartres, a Strasbourg, or a Durham mins-
ter, and in the mass, the pageant, the art gallery, the theater—
all this the Protestant bleached out into the bare abstraction of
the printed word. Did he suffer any hardship in moving to the
New World? None at all. All that he wanted of the Old World
he carried within the covers of a book. Fortunately for the original Protestants, that book was a whole literature; in this, at
least, it differed from the later protestant canons, perpetrated
by Joseph Smith or Mrs. Mary Baker Eddy. Unfortunately, however, the practices of a civilized society cannot be put between
two black covers. So, in some respects, Protestant society ceased
to be civilized.

III

Our critical eyes are usually a little dimmed by the great release of energy during the early Renaissance: we forget that it
quickly spent itself. For a little while the great humanists, such
as More, Erasmus, Scaliger, and Rabelais, created a new home
for the spirit out of the fragments of the past, and the new
thoughts were cemented together by the old habits of medieval
civilization, which persisted among the peasants and the crafts-
men, long after they had been undermined in the Church and
the palace.

The revival of classic culture, however, did not give men any
new power of command over the workaday routine of life, for
the very ability to reënter the past and have commerce with its
great minds implied leisure and scholarship. Thus the great
bulk of the community had no direct part in the revival, and if
the tailor or the tinker abandoned the established church, it was
only to espouse that segment called Protestantism. Tailors and
tinkers, almost by definition, could *not* be humanists. Moreover, beyond a certain point, humanism did not make connections with the new experience of the Columbuses and the New-
tons any better than did the medieval culture. If the criticism of
the pagan scholars released a good many minds from Catholic
theology, it did not orient them toward what was "new" and
"practical" and "coming." The Renaissance was not, therefore,

the launching out of a new epoch: it simply witnessed the break-down and disruption of the existing science, myth, and fable. When the Royal Society was founded in London in the middle of the Seventeenth Century the humanities were deliberately excluded. "Science" was indifferent to them.

Once the European, indeed, had abandoned the dream of medieval theology, he could not live very long on the memory of a classic culture: that, too, lost its meaning; that, too, failed to make connections with his new experiences in time and space. Leaving both behind him, he turned to what seemed to him a hard and patent reality: the external world. The old symbols, the old ways of living, had become a blank. Instead of them, he took refuge in abstractions, and reduced the rich actuality of things to a bare description of matter and motion. Along this path went the early scientists, or natural philosophers. By mathematical analysis and experiment, they extracted from the complicated totality of everyday experience just those phenomena which could be observed, measured, generalized, and, if necessary, repeated. Applying this exact methodology, they learned to predict more accurately the movements of the heavenly bodies, to describe more precisely the fall of a stone and the flight of a bullet, to determine the carrying load of a bridge, or the composition of a fragment of "matter." Rule, authority, precedent, general consent—these things were all subordinate in scientific procedure to the methods of observation and mathematical analysis: weighing, measuring, timing, decomposing, isolating—all operations that led to results.

At last knowledge could be tested and practice reformed; and if the scientists themselves were usually too busy to see the upshot of their investigations, one who stood on the sidelines, Francis Bacon, was quick to announce their conclusion: science tended to the relief of man's estate.

With the aid of this new procedure, the external world was quickly reduced to a semblance of order. But the meanings created by science did not lead into the core of human life: they applied only to "matter," and if they touched upon life at all, it was through a post-mortem analysis, or by following Descartes and arbitrarily treating the human organism as if it were auto-

matic and externally determined under all conditions. For the
scientists, these new abstractions were full of meaning and very
helpful; they tunneled through whole continents of knowledge.
For the great run of men, however, science had no meaning for
itself; it transferred meaning from the creature proper to his estate, considered as an independent and external realm. In short,
except to the scientist, the only consequences of science were
practical ones. A new view of the universe developed, naturally, but it was accepted less because of any innate credibility
than because it was accompanied by so many cogent proofs of
science's power. Philosophy, religion, art, none of these activities had ever baked any bread: science was ready, not merely to
bake the bread, but increase the yield of the wheat, grind the
flour and eliminate the baker. Even the plain man could appreciate consequences of this order. Seeing was believing. By the
middle of the Seventeenth Century all the implications of the
process had been imaginatively grasped. In 1661 Glanvill wrote:

"I doubt not posterity will find many things that are now but
rumors, verified into practical realities. It may be that, some
ages hence, a voyage to the Southern tracts, yea, possibly to the
moon, will not be more strange than one to America. To them
that come after us, it may be as ordinary to buy a pair of wings
to fly to remotest regions, as now a pair of boots to ride a journey; and to confer at the distance of the Indies by sympathetic
conveyances may be as usual in future times as by literary correspondence. The restoration of gray hairs to juvenility, and
renewing the exhausted marrow, may at length be effected without a miracle; and the turning of the now comparatively desert
world into a Paradise may not improbably be effected from late
agriculture."

IV

The process of abstraction began in the theology of Protestantism as an attempt to isolate, deform, and remove historic connections; it became habitual in the mental operations of the physical scientist; and it was carried over into other departments.

The extended use of money, to replace barter and service,
likewise began during this same period of disintegration. Need

I emphasize that in their origin Protestantism, physical science, and finance were all liberating influences? They took the place of habits and institutions which, plainly, were moribund, being incapable of renewal from within. Need I also emphasize the close historic inter-connection of the three things? We must not raise our eyebrows when we discover that a scientist like Newton in Seventeenth Century England, or Rittenhouse, in Eighteenth Century America, became master of the mint, nor must we pass by, as a quaint coincidence, the fact that Geneva is celebrated both as the home of Jean Calvin and as the great center of watches and clocks. These connections are not mystical nor factitious. The new financial order was a direct outgrowth of the new theological and scientific views. First came a mechanical method of measuring time: then a method of measuring space: finally, in money, men began more widely to apply an abstract way of measuring power, and in money they achieved a calculus for all human activity.

This financial system of measurement released the European from his old sense of social and economic limitations. No glutton can eat a hundred pheasants; no drunkard can drink a hundred bottles of wine at a sitting; and if any one schemed to have so much food and wine brought to his table daily, he would be mad. Once he could exchange the potential pheasants and Burgundy for marks or thalers, he could direct the labor of his neighbors, and achieve the place of an aristocrat without being to the manner born. Economic activity ceased to deal with the tangible realities of the medieval world—land and corn and houses and universities and cities. It was transformed into the pursuit of an abstraction—money. Tangible goods were only a means to this supreme end. When some incipient Rotarian finally coined the phrase, "Time is money," he expressed philosophically the equavalence of two ideas which could not possibly be combined, even in thought, so long as money meant houses, food, pictures, and time meant only what it does in Bergson's *durée,* that is, the succession of organic experiences.

Does all this seem very remote from the common life? On the contrary, it goes to the roots of every activity. The difference between historical periods, as the late T. E. Hulme pointed out,

is a difference between the categories of their thought. If we
have got on the trail of their essential categories, we have a
thread which will lead outward into even remote departments of
life. The fact is that from the Seventeenth Century onward, almost every field was invaded by this process of abstraction. The
people not affected were either survivals from an older epoch,
like the orthodox Jews and Roman Catholics in theology, or
the humanists in literature, or they were initiators, working
through to a new order—men like Lamarck, Wordsworth,
Goethe, Comte.

Last and most plainly of all, the disintegration of medieval
culture became apparent in politics. Just as "matter," when examined by the physicist is abstracted from the esthetic matrix of
our experience, so the "individual" was abstracted by the political philosopher of the new order from the bosom of human society. He ceased, this individual, to maintain his omnipresent
relations with city, family, household, club, college, guild, and
office: he became the new unit of political society. Having abstracted this purely conceptual person in thought—he had, of
course, no more actual existence than an angel or a cherub—the
great problem of political thinking in the Eighteenth Century
became: How shall we restore him to society?—for somehow
we always find man, as Rousseau grimly said, in chains, that is,
in relations with other human beings. The solution that Rousseau and the dominant schools of the time offered was ingenious:
each individual is endowed with natural rights, and he votes
these political rights into society, as the shareholder votes his
economic rights into a trading corporation. This principle of
consent was necessary to the well-being of a civil society; and as-
sent was achieved, in free political states, through the operation
of the ballot, and the delivery of the general will by a parlia-
ment.

The doctrine broke the weakening chain of historical continuity in Europe. It challenged the vested interests; it was ready to
declare the existing corporations bankrupt; it was prepared to
wipe away the traditional associations and nets of privileges
which maintained the clergy, the nobility, the guilds. On its de-
structive side, the movement for political liberty, like that for

free contract, free association, and free investigation, was sane and reasonable; for the abuses of the past were genuine and the grievances usually had more than a small touch of justice. We must not, however, be blind to the consequences of all these displacements and dissociations. Perhaps the briefest way of characterizing them is to say that they made America inevitable. To those who were engaged in political criticism, it seemed that a genuine political order had been created in the setting up of free institutions; but we can see now that the process was an inevitable bit of surgery, rather than the beginning of a more organic form of political association. By 1852 Henry James, Sr., was keen enough to see what had happened: "Democracy," he observed, "is not so much a new form of political life as a dissolution and disorganization of the old forms. It is simply a resolution of government into the hands of the people, a taking down of that which has before existed, and a recommitment of it to its original sources, but it is by no means the substitution of anything else in its place."

V

Now we begin to see a little more clearly the state of mind out of which the great migrations to the New World became possible. The physical causes have been dwelt on often enough; it is important to recognize that a cultural necessity was at work at the same time. The old culture of the Middle Ages had broken down; the old heritage lingered on only in the "backward" and "unprogressive" countries like Italy and Spain, which drifted outside the main currents of the European mind. Men's interests became externalized; externalized and abstract. They fixed their attention on some narrow aspect of experience, and they pushed that to the limit. Intelligent people were forced to choose between the fossilized shell of an old and complete culture, and the new culture, which in origin was thin, partial, abstract, and deliberately indifferent to man's proper interests. Choosing the second, our Europeans already had one foot in America. Let them suffer persecution, let the times get hard, let them fall out with their governments, let them dream of worldly success—and they will come swarming over the ocean.

The groups that had most completely shaken off the old symbol-
isms were those that were most ready for the American adventure: they turned themselves easily to the mastery of the external environment. To them matter alone mattered.

The ultimate results of this disintegration of European culture did not come out, in America, until the Nineteenth Century. But its immediate consequence became visible, step by
step, in the first hundred and fifty years or so of the American
settlement. Between the landing of the first colonists in Massachusetts, the New Netherlands, Virginia and Maryland, and the
first thin trickle of hunters that passed over the Alleghenies, beginning figuratively with Daniel Boone in 1775, the communities of the Atlantic seaboard were outposts of Europe: they carried their own moral and intellectual climate with them.

During this period, the limitations in the thought of the intellectual classes had not yet wrought themselves out into defects
and malformations in the community itself: the house, the
town, the farm were still modeled after patterns formed in Europe. It was not a great age, perhaps, but it had found its form.
Walking through the lanes of Boston, or passing over the wide
lawns to a manor house in Maryland, one would have had no
sense of a great wilderness beckoning in the beyond. To tell the
truth, the wilderness did not beckon: these solid townsmen,
these freeholders, these planters, were content with their civil
habits; and if they thought of expansion, it was only over the
ocean, in search of Palladian designs for their houses, or of tea
and sperm-oil for their personal comfort. On the surface, people
lived as they had lived in Europe for many a year.

In the first century of colonization, this life left scarcely any
deposit in the mind. There was no literature but a handful of
verses, no music except the hymn or some surviving Elizabethan ballad, no ideas except those that circled around the dog-
mas of Protestantism. But, with the Eighteenth Century, these
American communities stepped fully into the sphere of European ideas, and there was an American equivalent for every new
European type. It is amusing to follow the leading biographies
of the time. Distinguished American figures step onto the stage,
in turn, as if the Muse of History had prepared their entrances

and exits. Their arrangement is almost diagrammatic: they form a résumé of the European mind. In fact, these Edwardses and Franklins seem scarcely living characters: they were Protestantism, Science, Finance, Politics.

The first on the stage was Jonathan Edwards: he figured in American thought as the last great expositor of Calvinism. Edwards wrote like a man in a trance, who at bottom is aware that he is talking nonsense; for he was in love with beauty of the soul, like Plato before him, and it was only because he was caught in the premises of determinism that, with a heavy conscience, he followed his dire train of thought to its destination. After Edwards, Protestantism lost its intellectual backbone. It developed into the bloodless Unitarianism of the early Nineteenth Century, which is a sort of humanism without courage, or it got caught in orgies of revivalism, and, under the name of evangelical Christianity, threw itself under the hoofs of more than one muddy satyr. There were great Protestant preachers after Edwards, no doubt: but the triumph of a Channing or a Beecher rested upon personal qualities; and they no longer drew their thoughts from any deep well of conviction.

All the habits that Protestantism developed, its emphasis upon industry, upon self-help, upon thrift, upon the evils of "idleness" and "pleasure," upon the worldliness and wickedness of the arts, were so many gratuitous contributions to the industrial revolution. When Professor Morse, the inventor of the telegraph, was still a painter, traveling in Italy, he recorded in one of his letters the animus that pervaded his religious creed: the testimony loses nothing by being a little belated. "I looked around the church," he wrote, "to ascertain what was the effect upon the multitude assembled. . . . Everything around them, instead of aiding devotion, was entirely calculated to destroy it. The imagination was addressed by every avenue; music and painting pressed into the service of—not religion but the contrary—led the mind away from the contemplation of all that is practical in religion to the charms of mere sense. No instruction was imparted; none ever seems to be intended."

It is but a short step from this attitude to hiring revivalist mountebanks to promote factory morale; nor are these thoughts

far from that fine combination of commercial zeal and pious effort which characterize such auxiliaries as the Y. M. C. A.
The fictions of poetry and the delusions of feeling were the bug-
bears of Gradgrind, Bounderby, and M'Choakumchild in Dick-
ens's classic picture of industrialism: for the shapes and images
they called forth made those which were familiar to the Protestant mind a little dreary and futile. It was not merely that Protestantism and science had killed the old symbols: they must
prevent new ones from developing: they must abolish the contemplative attitude in which art and myth grow up, and create
new forms for man's activities. Hence the fury of effort by
which the leaders of the new day diverted energies to quantitative production. The capacity to do work, which the new methods in industry had so enormously increased, gave utilitarian objects an importance they had not hitherto possessed. Did not
God's Word say: "Increase and multiply"? If babies, why not
goods: if goods, why not dollars? Success was the Protestant
miracle that justified man's ways to God.

The next figure that dominated the American scene stood
even more completely for these new forces. He was, according
to the pale lights of his time, a thoroughly cultivated man, and
in his maturity he was welcomed in London and Paris as the
equal of scientists like Priestley and Erasmus Darwin, and of
scholars like d'Alembert and d'Holbach. As a citizen, by choice,
of Philadelphia, Benjamin Franklin adopted the plain manners
and simple thrifty ways of the Quakers. He went into business
as a publisher, and with a sort of sweet acuteness in the pursuit
of money, he imparted the secrets of his success in the collection
of timely saws for which he became famous. The line from
Franklin through Samuel Smiles to the latest advertisements for
improving one's position and doubling one's income, in the pa-
per that dates back to Franklin's ownership, is a pretty direct
one. If one prefers Franklin's bourgeois qualities to those of
his successors, it is only perhaps because his life was more fully
rounded. If he was not without the usurious habits of the financier, he had also the dignity and freedom of the true scientist.

For Franklin was equally the money-maker, the scientist, the
inventor, and the politician, and in science his fair boast was

that he had not gained a penny by any of his discoveries. He experimented with electricity; he invented the lightning rod; he improved the draft of chimneys; in fact, on his last voyage home to America, shortly before his death, he was still improving the draft of chimneys. Finally he was a Deist: he had gotten rid of all the "gothick phantoms" that seemed so puerile and unworthy to the quick minds of the Eighteenth Century—which meant that he was completely absorbed in the dominant abstractions and myths of his own time, namely, matter, money, and political rights. He accepted the mechanical concept of time: time is money; the importance of space: space must be conquered; the desirability of money: money must be made; and he did not see that these, too, are phantoms, in preoccupation with which a man may lose most of the advantages of a civilized life. As a young man, Franklin even invented an elaborate system of moral-bookkeeping: utilitarianism can go no further.

Although Franklin's sagacity as a statesman can hardly be overrated, for he had both patience and principle, the political side of the American thought of his time is best summed up in the doctrines of a new immigrant, that excellent friend of humanity, Thomas Paine. Paine's name has served so many purposes in polemics that scarcely any one seems to take the trouble to read his books: and so more than one shallow judgment has found its way into our histories of literature, written by worthy men who were incapable of enjoying a sound English style, or of following, with any pleasure, an honest system of thought, clearly expressed. The Rights of Man is as simple as a geometrical theorem; it contains, I think, most of what is valid in political libertarianism. I know of no other thinker who saw more clearly through the moral humbug that surrounds a good many theories of government. Said Paine:

"Almost everything appertaining to the circumstances of a nation has been absorbed and confounded under the general and mysterious word government. Though it avoids taking to its account the errors it commits and the mischiefs it occasions, it fails not to arrogate to itself whatever has the appearance of prosperity. It robs industry of its honors by pedantically making itself the cause of its effects; and purloins from the general character of man the merits that appertain to him as a social being."

Passage after passage in The Rights of Man and The Age of Reason is written with the same pithiness. Paine came to America as an adult, and saw the advantages of a fresh start. He believed that if first principles could be enunciated, here, and here alone, was a genuine opportunity to apply them. He summed up the hope in reason and in human contrivance that swelled through the Eighteenth Century. Without love for any particular country, and without that living sense of history which makes one accept the community's past, as one accepts the totality of one's own life, with all its lapses and mistakes, he was the vocal immigrant, justifying in his political and religious philosophy the complete break he had made with old ties, affections, allegiances.

Unfortunately, a man without a background is not more truly a man: he has merely lost the scenes and institutions which gave him his proper shape. If one studies him closely, one will find that he has secretly arranged another background, made up of shadows that linger in the memory, or he is uneasy and restless, settles down, moves on, comes home again, lives on hopeless to-morrows, or sinks back into mournful yesterdays. The immigrants who came to America after the War of Independence gave up their fatherland in exchange for a Constitution and a Bill of Rights: they forfeited all the habits and institutions which had made them men without getting anything in exchange except freedom from arbitrary misrule. That they made the exchange willingly, proves that the conditions behind them were intolerable; but that the balance was entirely in favor of the new country, is something that we may well doubt. When the new settlers migrated in bodies, like the Moravians, they sometimes managed to maintain an effective cultural life; when they came alone, as "free individuals," they gained little more than cheap land and the privileges of the ballot box. The land itself was all to the good; and no one minded the change, or felt any lack, so long as he did not stop to compare the platitudes of Fourth of July orations with the actualities of the Slave Trade, the Constitutional Conventions, Alien and Sedition Acts, and Fugitive Slave Laws.

It was possible for Paine, in the Eighteenth Century, to believe that culture was served merely by the absence of a church, a state, a social order such as those under which Europe labored. That was the error of his school, for the absence of these harmful or obsolete institutions left a vacancy in society, and that vacancy was filled by work, or more accurately speaking, by busy work, which fatigued the body and diverted the mind from the things which should have enriched it. Republican politics aided this externalism. People sought to live by politics alone; the National State became their religion. The flag, as Professor Carleton Hayes has shown, supplanted the cross, and the Fathers of the Constitution the Fathers of the Church.

The interaction of the dominant interests of industry and politics is illustrated in Paine's life as well as Franklin's. Paine was the inventor of the take-down iron bridge. Indeed, politics and invention recurred rhythmically in his life, and he turned aside from his experiments on the iron bridge to answer Edmund Burke's attack on the French Revolution. "The War of Independence," as he himself said, "energized invention and lessened the catalogue of impossibilities. . . . As one among thousands who had borne a share in that memorable revolution, I returned with them to the enjoyment of a quiet life, and that I might not be idle, undertook to construct a bridge of a single arch for this river [the Schuylkill]."

That I might not be idle! What a tale those words tell! While the aristocracy was in the ascendant, patient hirelings used to apply their knowledge of hydraulics to the working of fountains, as in Versailles, or they devised automatic chess-players, or they contrived elaborate clocks which struck the hour, jetted water, caused little birds to sing and wag their tails, and played selections from the operas. It was to such inane and harmless performances that the new skills in the exact arts were first put. The bored patron was amused; life plodded on; nothing was altered. But in the freedom of the new day, the common man, as indifferent to the symbols of the older culture as the great lords and ladies, innocent of anything to occupy his mind, except the notion of controlling matter and mastering the external world—the common man turned to inventions. Stupid folk drank heavily, ate gluttonously, and became libertines; intelligent, industrious men like Franklin and Paine, turned their minds to increasing the comforts and conveniences of existence. Justification by faith: that was politics: the belief in a new heaven and a new earth to be established by regular elections and parliamentary debate. Justification by works: that was invention. No frivolities entered this new religion. The new devices all saved labor, decreased distances, and in one way or another multiplied riches.

With these inventors, the American, like his contemporary in Europe, began the utilitarian conquest of his environment. From this time on, men with an imaginative bias like Morse, the pupil of Benjamin West, men like Whitney, the school-teacher, like Fulton, the miniature painter, turned to invention or at least the commercial exploitation of inventions without a qualm of distrust: to abandon the imaginative arts seemed natural and inevitable, and they no longer faced the situation, as the painters of the Renaissance had done, with a divided mind. Not that America began or monopolized the developments of the Industrial Revolution: the great outbreak of technical patents began, in fact, in England about 1760, and the first inklings of the movement were already jotted down in Leonardo da Vinci's notebooks. The point is that in Europe heavy layers of the old culture kept large sections of the directing classes in the old ways. Scholars, literary men, historians, artists still felt no need of justifying themselves by exclusive devotion to practical activities. In America, however, the old culture had worn thin, and in the rougher parts of the country it did not exist. No one in America was unaffected by the progress of invention; each improvement was quickly cashed in. When Stendhal wrote L'Amour the American love of comfort had already become a by-word: he refers to it with contempt.

Given an old culture in ruins, and a new culture *in vacuo,* this externalizing of interest, this ruthless exploitation of the physical environment was, it would seem, inevitable. Protestantism, science, invention, political democracy, all of these institutions denied the old values; all of them, by denial or by precept or by actual absorption, furthered the new activities. Thus in America the new order of Europe came quickly into being. If the Nineteenth Century found us more raw and rude, it was not because we had settled in a new territory; it was rather because our minds were not buoyed up by all those memorials of a great past that floated over the surface of Europe. The American was thus a stripped European; and the colonization of America can, with justice, be called the dispersion of Europe—a movement carried on by people incapable of sharing or continuing its past. It was to America that the outcast Europeans turned, without a Moses to guide them, to wander in the wilderness; and here they have remained in exile, not without an occasional glimpse, perhaps, of the promised land.

Chapter Two The Romanticism
of the Pioneer

I

THE pioneer has usually been looked upon as a typical product of the American environment; but the truth is that he existed in the European mind before he made his appearance here. Pioneering may in part be described as the Romantic movement in action. If one wishes to fathom the pioneer's peculiar behavior, one must not merely study his relations with the Indians, with the trading companies, and with the government's land policies: one must also understand the main currents of European thought in the Eighteenth Century. In the episode of pioneering, a new system of ideas wedded itself to a new set of experiences: the experiences were American, but the ideas themselves had been nurtured in Savoy, in the English lake country, and on the Scots moors. Passing into action, these ideas became queerly transmogrified, so that it now takes more than a little digging to see the relation between Chateaubriand and Mark Twain, or Rousseau and William James. The pioneer arose out of an external opportunity, an unopened continent, and out of an inward necessity. It is the inward necessity that most of our commentators upon him have neglected.

In the Eighteenth Century, Europe became at last conscious of the fact that the living sources of its older culture had dried up; and it made its first attempt to find a basis for a new culture. Many of its old institutions were already hollow and rotten. The guilds had become nests of obsolete privileges, which stood doggedly in the way of any technical improvement. The church, in England and in France, had become an institution for providing support to the higher ranks of the clergy, who believed only in the mundane qualities of bread and wine. In

fact, all the remains of medieval Europe were in a state of piti-
able decay; they were like venerable apple trees, burgeoned
with suckers and incapable of bearing fruit. A mere wind
would have been enough to send the old structure toppling;
instead of it, a veritable tempest arose, and by the time Voltaire
had finished with the Church, Montesquieu and Rousseau
with the State, Turgot and Adam Smith with the old corporations, there was scarcely anything left that an intelligent man
of the Eighteenth Century would have cared to carry away.
Once the old shelters and landmarks were gone, where could
people turn? The classic past had already been tried, and had
been found—dull. Medievalism was not yet quite dead enough
to be revived; *chinoiseries* were merely amusing. There remained one great and permanent source of culture, and with a
hundred different gestures the Eighteenth Century acclaimed it
—Nature.

The return to Nature occurred at the very climax of an arranged and artificial existence: trees had been clipped, hedges
had been deformed, architecture had become as cold and fin-
icking as a pastrycook's icing, the very hair of the human head
had been exchanged for the white wig of senility. Precisely at
this moment, when a purely urbane convention seemed established forever, a grand retreat began. In the Middle Ages such
a retreat would have led to the monastery: it now pushed back
to the country, by valiant mountain paths, like Rousseau's, or
by mincing little country lanes, like that which led Marie
Antoinette to build an English village in Versailles, and play
at being a milkmaid. Nature was the fashion: "every one did
it." If one had resources, one laid out a landscape park, wild
like the fells of Yorkshire, picturesque like the hills of Cumber-
land, the whole atmosphere heightened by an artificial ruin, to
show dramatically the dominance of Nature over man's puny
handiwork. If one were middle class, one built a villa, called
Idle Hour, or The Hermitage; at the very least, one took country walks, or dreamed of a superb adventurous manhood in
America.

In the mind of the great leader of this movement, Jean-
Jacques Rousseau, Nature was not a fresh element in the tissue

of European culture: it was a complete substitute for the existing institutions, conventions, habits, and histories. Rousseau
began his career with an essay on the question whether the restoration of the arts and sciences had the effect of purifying or
corrupting public morals: he won the prize offered by the acad-
emy at Dijon by affirming their tendency to corrupt; and from
that time onward (1750) he continued to write, with better
sense but with hardly any decrease in his turbulent conviction,
upon the worthlessness of contemporary civilization in Europe.
His prescription was simple: return to Nature: shun society:
enjoy solitude. Rousseau's Nature was not Newton's Nature—
a system of matter and motion, ordered by Providence, and established in the human mind by nice mathematical calcula-
tions. By Nature Rousseau meant the mountains, like those
which shoulder across the background of his birthplace; he
meant the mantle of vegetation, where one might botanize, and
see "eternity in a grain of sand, and heaven in a wild flower;"
he meant the fields, like those of Savoy, where a simple peas-
antry practiced the elementary routine of living.

The return to Nature, in Rousseau's sense, was not a new in-
junction; nor was it an unsound one. As an aid to recovery in
physical illness and neurosis, its value was recognized at least
as early as Hippocrates, and as a general social formula it has
played a part in the life and literature of every finished civilization. The Georgics, the Bucolics, and the idylls of classic culture belong to its sophisticated moments: after the formalities
of the Confucian period Lao-tse's philosophy developed a similar creed and persuaded its individualistic adherents to re-
nounce the sterile practices of the court and the bureaucracy
and bury themselves in the Bamboo Grove. Nature almost inevitably becomes dominant in the mind when the powers of
man himself to mold his fortunes and make over his institutions
seem feeble—when, in order to exist at all, it is necessary to accept the wilderness of Nature and human passion as "given,"
without trying to subdue its disorder.

What made the authority of Rousseau's doctrine so immense,
what made it play such a presiding part in European life, echoing through the minds of Goethe, Herder, Kant, Wordsworth,

and even, quite innocently, Blake, was the fact that there awaited the European in America a Nature that was primitive and undefiled. In the purely mythical continent that uprose in the European mind, the landscape was untainted by human blood and tears, and the Red Indian, like Atala, led a life of physical dignity and spiritual austerity: the great Sachem was an aborigine with the stoic virtues of a Marcus Aurelius. Rousseau's glorification of peasant life was after all subject to scrutiny, and by the time the French Revolution came, the peasant had a word or two to say about it himself; but the true child of Nature in the New World, uncorrupted by the superstitions of the Church, could be idealized to the heart's content: his customs could be attributed to the unhindered spontaneity of human nature, his painfully acquired and transmitted knowledge might be laid to instinctive processes; in short, he became a pure ideal. Even William Blake could dream of liberty on the banks of the Ohio, if not on the banks of the Thames.

In America, if society was futile, one had only to walk half a day to escape it; in Europe, if one walked half a day one would be in the midst of another society. In Europe one had to *plan* a retreat: in America one simply encountered it. If Nature was, as Wordsworth said, a world of ready wealth, blessing our minds and hearts with wisdom and health and cheerfulness, what place could be richer than America? Once Romanticism turned its eyes across the ocean, it became a movement indeed. It abandoned culture to return to Nature; it left a skeleton of the past for an embryo of the future; it renounced its hoarded capital and began to live on its current income; it forfeited the old and the tried for the new and the experimental. This transformation was, as Nietzsche said, an immense physiological process, and its result was "the slow emergence of an essentially super-national and nomadic species of man, who possesses, physiologically speaking, a maximum of the art and power of adaptation as his typical distinction."

The Romantic Movement was thus the great formative influence which produced not merely the myth of pioneering, but the pioneer. But it was not the sole influence upon the scene. Human society was divided in the Eighteenth Century between

those who thought it perfectible, and those who thought that
the existing institutions were all essentially rotten: the Ben-
thams and the Turgots were on one side, the Rousseaus and
Blakes on the other, and the great mass of people mixed these
two incompatible doctrines in varying proportions. The per-
fectionists believed in progress, science, laws, education, and
comfort; progress was the mode and comfort the end of every
civil arrangement. The followers of Rousseau believed in none
of these things. Instead of sense, they wanted sensibility; instead of education, spontaneity; instead of smokeless chimneys
and glass windows and powerlooms, a clear sky and an open
field.

If the pioneer was the lawfully begotten child of the Romantic Movement, he belonged to the other school by adoption.
He wanted Nature; and he wanted comfort no less. He sought
to escape the conventions of society; yet his notion of a free
government was one that devoted itself to a perpetual process
of legislation, and he made no bones about appealing to the
Central Government when he wanted inland waterways and
roads and help in exterminating the Indian. Society was effete:
its machinery could be perfected—the pioneer accepted both
these notions. He believed with Rousseau that "man is good
naturally, and that by institutions only is he made bad." And
if the Yankees who first settled in Illinois were looked upon as
full of "notions" because they were wont to take thought for
the morrow and to multiply mechanical devices, these habits,
too, were quickly absorbed. As Nature grew empty, progress
took its place in the mind of the pioneer. Each of these ideas
turned him from the past, and enabled him to speculate, in
both the commercial and philosophic senses of the word, on the
future.

II

In America the return to nature set in before there was any
physical necessity for filling up the raw lands of the West. The
movement across the Alleghanies began long before the East
was fully occupied: it surged up in the third quarter of the
Eighteenth Century, after the preliminary scouting and road-

building by the Ohio Company, and by the time the Nineteenth Century was under way, the conquest of the Continent
had become the obsession of every progressive American community.

This westward expansion of the pioneer was, without doubt,
furthered by immediate causes, such as the migration of dis-
banded soldiers after the Revolution, endowed with land-war-
rants; but from the beginning, the movement was compulsive
and almost neurotic; and as early as 1837 Peck's New Guide to
the West recorded that "migration has become almost a habit."
External matters of fact would perhaps account for the New
England migration to Ohio: they cease to be relevant, however,
when they are called upon to explain the succession of jumps
which caused so many settlers to pull up stakes and move into
Illinois—and then into Missouri—and so beyond, until finally
the Pacific Coast brought the movement temporarily to an end.
This restless search was something more than a prospecting of
resources; it was an experimental investigation of Nature, Solitude, The Primitive Life; and at no stage of the journey, however much the story may be obscured by land-booms and Indian massacres and gold rushes, did these things drop out of the
pioneer's mind. Charles Fenno Hoffman in A Winter in the
West (1835), was only echoing the unconscious justification of
the pioneer when he exclaimed: "What is the echo of roofs
that a few centuries since rung with barbaric revels, or of aisles
that pealed the anthems of painted pomp, to the silence which
has reigned in these dim groves since the first fiat of Creation
was spoken?"

Mark the difference between this movement and that which
first planted the colonists of Massachusetts or Pennsylvania in
the New World. In the first period of the seaboard settlement,
America was a place where the European could remain more
nearly his proper self, and keep up the religious practices which
were threatened by economic innovations and political infringe-
ments in Europe. The Puritans, the Moravians, the Dunkers,
the Quakers, the Catholics, sought America as a refuge in
which they could preserve in greater security what they dearly
valued in Europe. But with the drift to the West, America be-

came, on the contrary, a place where the European could be swiftly transformed into something different: where the civil man could become a hardy savage, where the social man could become an "individual," where the settled man could become a nomad, and the family man could forget his old connections. With pioneering, America ceased to be an outpost of Europe. The Western communities relapsed into an earlier and more primitive type of occupation; they reverted to the crude practices of the hunter, the woodman, and the miner. Given the occasion and the environment, these were necessary occupations; the point to be noted, however, is that, uninfluenced by peasant habits or the ideas of an old culture, the work of the miner, woodman, and hunter led to unmitigated destruction and pillage. What happened was just the reverse of the old barbarian invasions, which turned the Goths and the Vandals into Romans. The movement into backwoods America turned the European into a barbarian.

The grisly process of this settlement was described by Crève-cœur and Cooper long before Professor Turner summed them up in his classic treatise on the passing of the frontier. "In all societies," says Crèvecœur, "there are off-casts; this impure part serves as our precursors or pioneers. . . . By living in or near the woods, their actions are regulated by the neighborhood. The deer often come to eat their grain, the wolves to destroy their sheep, the bears to kill their hogs, the foxes to catch their poultry. The surrounding hostility immediately puts the gun into their hands; they watch these animals; they kill some; and thus, by defending their property, they soon become professed hunters; this is the progress; once hunters, farewell to the plow. The chase renders them ferocious, gloomy, unsociable; a hunter wants no neighbors, he rather hates them because he dreads competition."

Equipped with his ax and his rifle, the two principal weapons of the pioneer, he carried on his warfare against Nature, cutting down the forest and slaughtering its living creatures. Instead of seeking Nature in a wise passiveness, as Wordsworth urged, he raped his new mistress in a blind fury of obstreperous passion. No one who has read The Pioneers can forget

Cooper's account of the sickening massacre of wild pigeons, carried on long after the need for food had been satisfied. In these practices, the ordinary farmer and tradesman of the old country went back to a phase of European experience which had lingered on chiefly in the archaic hunts of a predatory aristocracy; and in the absence of any restraints or diversions, these primitive practices sank more deeply into the grain.

The apology for this behavior was based upon the noblest grounds; one can scarcely pick up a contemporary description of the pioneering period without finding a flowery account of the new life, put in contrast to wretched, despotic, foolishly beautiful Europe; and this animus was echoed even in the comments that Hawthorne and Emerson, to say nothing of such a real pioneer as Mark Twain, made upon the institutions of the Old World. Let me put the contemporary apology and criticism side by side. The first is from a pamphlet by George Lunt called Three Eras of New England (1857):

"Whenever this is the state of man the impertinent fictions and sophisms of life die out. The borrowings and lendings of the human creature fall away from him under the rigid discipline of primeval necessities, as the encrusting dirt, which bedimmed the diamond, is removed by the hard process which reveals and confirms its inestimable price. The voice of the mountain winds would mock at the most indispensable and best recognized trappings of polished society as they rent them away and fastened them fluttering in the crevices of a cliff, or bore them onwards to the unknown wilderness, and would hail its very discomforts with the shout and laughter of derision. . . . So far, therefore, as our familiar and inherent characteristics, which form the foundation of our nature, and make us good and make us great, are liable to become diluted or perverted by the sophistications of social being, they may require an actual refreshment and renewal, under the severe and inevitable trials of colonial existence. . . . This, then, is the absolute law of all legitimate migration, that it leaves behind it the weaknesses, the concretions and superfluities of artificial life, and founds its new existence upon an appeal to the primordial elements of natural society."

Against this apology for the deprivations of the pioneer life, let me set the comment of a young English settler named Fordham, who had come face to face with the untrammeled Children of Nature; this passage occurs on the page after that in which he records the amiable slaughter of six Indians, men and women, on English Prairie, in the spring of 1817:

"Instead of being more virtuous, as he is less refined, I am inclined to think that man's virtues are like the fruits of the earth, only excellent when subjected to culture. The force of the simile you will never feel, until you ride in these woods over wild strawberries, which dye your horses' fetlocks like blood, yet are insipid in flavour; till you have seen wagon-loads of grapes, choked by the brambles and the poisonous vine; till you find peaches, tasteless as a turnip, and roses throwing their leaves of every shade upon the wind, with scarcely a scent upon them. 'Tis the hand of man that makes the wilderness shine."

The hand of man was of course busy, and here and there, particularly in Ohio, Kentucky and Tennessee, villages and cities grew up which carried on, for a generation or so in the Nineteenth Century, the tradition that the seaboard knew in an earlier day; but like a river that, rushing onwards, deposits its heaviest burdens first, the best people and the soundest traditions tended to be deposited in the tracts that adjoined the original colonies, and as the stream moved further west, the traditions of a civil life disappeared, and the proportion of scalawags, cut-throats, bruisers, bullies, and gamblers tended to increase, and the wilderness got the upper hand. There are plenty of exceptions to this generalization, it goes without saying; but Texas and Nevada were the poles towards which pioneer effort tended to run. The original process has been obscured in many places by a second and third wave of agriculturists: but it is not hard to get below the surface and see what the original reality was.

III

The shock of the pioneer's experience left its mark in one or two gestures of anticipation, and in an aftermath of regretful reminiscence. The post-Civil War writers who deal with

Roughing It, A Son of the Middle Border, or A Hoosier School-master, to mention only a few examples, had already abandoned the scene of the pioneer's efforts and had returned to the East: they made copy of their early life, but, though they might be inclined to sigh after it, because it was associated with their youth, they had only a sentimental notion of continuing it. For them, the pioneering experience could be recapitulated in a night around a camp-fire or a visit to the Wild West Show, which the astute Barnum had introduced to the denizens of New York in a day when the West was still in fact wild. A genuine culture and a relevant way of life do not lose their significance so easily; and the thin-skinnedness of the pioneer in the face of criticism, and the eagerness of the post-pioneer generation—The Inheritors of Susan Glaspell's play—to identify themselves with the culture of the past, shows, I think, that at bottom the pioneer realized that his efforts had gone awry.

One is faced by the paradox that the formative elements in the pioneer's career expressed themselves in literature almost at the very outset of the movement, in the works of men who were in fact almost as aloof from the realities of the western exodus as Chateaubriand himself; and although the pioneer types and the pioneer adventures have been repeated in literature of the rubber-stamp pattern from Gustave Aimard to Zane Grey, what was valid and what was peculiar in the pioneer regime was embodied, once for all, by James Fenimore Cooper. These new contacts, these new scenes, these adventures, served to create just three genuine folk-heroes. In these heroes, the habits of the pioneer were raised to the plane of a pattern.

Cooper's Leatherstocking was the new *Natur-Mensch*, established on a platform of simple human dignity. He was versed in the art of the woods, with the training of the aborigine himself; he shared the reticence and shyness that the Amerind perhaps showed in the company of strangers; and above the tender heart he exhibited mutely in The Deerslayer, he disclosed a leathery imperturbability. His eye was unerring; and it was only in instinct that Chingachgook, the Indian, sometimes surpassed this great hunter and warrior. Leatherstocking's bullet, which drives the bullet that has already hit the bull's eye still deeper into the target, is of course no ordinary bullet: it shared the inevitable enlargement of the hero's powers. Not every pioneer, needless to say, was a Natty Bumppo; but the shy, reserved, taciturn, dryly humorous hunter was the sort of being the pioneer tended, under the first stress of his new association, to become. Cooper himself painted other pioneer types, the sullen squatter, Ishmael, the fur trader, the frontier soldier, the woodman, the bee-hunter; but the fact that he had already outlined the character of Leatherstocking in the equally shrewd and reserved Spy of the Neutral Ground, Harvey Birch, showed, I believe, that this figure had become a property of his unconscious.

First a hunter, then a scout, then a trapper, Leatherstocking encompassed the chief pioneering experiences; it required a generation or two before the trader became the boomtown manufacturer, and the manufacturer the realtor and financier, dealing only with the tokens of industry. Like the first pioneers, Leatherstocking fled before the smoke of the settler's domestic fire, as before the prairie fire itself. With all the shoddiness of Cooper's imaginative constructions, he was plainly seized by a great character: his novels live solely through their central conception of Leatherstocking. The hard man, a Sir Giles Overreach, or the cunning man, Ulysses, had been portrayed before in literature; but the hardness and craft of Leatherstocking brought forth a new quality, which came directly from the woods and the prairies. When the pioneer called his first political hero Old Hickory he poetically expressed this new truth of character: barbarians or outlaws they might be, these pioneers, but their heroes grew straight. This straightness is the great quality one feels in Lincoln. It was as if, after centuries of clipping and pruning, we had at last allowed a tree to grow to its full height, shaped only by snow, rain, sun, wind, frost. A too timid and complacent culture may sacrifice the inner strength to an agreeable conformity to a common mold, a little undersized. These Old Hickories, on the other hand, grew a little scraggly and awkward; but in their reach, one would catch, occasionally, a hint of the innate possibilities of the species.

In the course of the Nineteenth Century, Leatherstocking was joined by an even more authentic folk hero, Paul Bunyan, whose gigantic shape, partly perhaps derived from Gargantua through his French-Canadian forebears, took form over the fire in the logger's shack. Paul Bunyan, properly enough, was an axman; and, as if to complete the symbolism and identify himself more completely with the prime activities of the new American type, he was also a great inventor. He figures on a continental scale. All his prowess and strength is based upon the notion that a thing becomes a hundred times as important if it is a hundred times as big. The habit of counting and "calculating" and "figuring" and "reckoning" and "guessing"—the habit, that is, of exchanging quality for number—is expressed in nearly all of Bunyan's exploits. In a day when no one dared point to the string of shacks that formed the frontier town as a proof of the qualitative beauties and delights of a pioneer community, the popular imagination took refuge in a statistical criterion of value: they counted heads: they counted money: they counted miles: they counted anything that lent itself to large figures.

This habit grew to such an extent that people began to appreciate its comic quality; in the Bunyan tales it is a device of humor as well as of heroic exaggeration. For many years, as the legend was quietly growing and expanding, Paul Bunyan lurked under the surface of our life: we lived by his light, even if we were ignorant of his legend. He, too, like Leatherstocking, was aloof from women; and this fact is not without significance; for with the woman the rough bachelor life must come to an end, and though the pioneer might carry his family with him, bedstead, baby, and all, they were sooner or later bound to domesticate him, and make him settle down. Woman was the chief enemy of the pioneer: she courageously rose to the burdens of the new life, and demanded her place side by side in the legislature: but in the end she had her revenge, in temperance clubs, in anti-vice societies, or in the general tarnation tidiness of Tom Sawyer's aunt. When Whitman sang of the Perfect Comrade, he did not at first think of woman: so far from indicating a special sexual anomaly in Whitman, it is

rather a tribute to his imaginative identification with the col-
lective experience of his generation.

At the same time, another folk-hero arose in literature, at
first sight an incomprehensible one. He was neither heroic,
nor, on the surface, a pioneer; and the story that brought him
forth was a rather commonplace fantasy of an earlier day. Yet
the history of Rip Van Winkle shows that he has had a deep
hold on the American mind: Irving's tale itself remains a popular legend, and the play that was written about him as early as
the eighteen-thirties was remodeled by succeeding generations
of American actors, until given its classic form by Joseph Jefferson. How did this happen? The reason, I think, was that
Rip's adventures and disappointments stood for that of the
typical American of the pioneer period. Inept at consecutive
work, harried by his wife, and disgusted with human society,
he retires to the hills with his dog and his gun. He drinks heavily, falls asleep, and becomes enchanted. At the end of twenty
years he awakes to find himself in a different society. The old
landmarks have gone; the old faces have disappeared; all the
outward aspects of life have changed. At the bottom, however,
Rip himself has not changed; for he has been drunk and lost
in a dream, and for all that the calendar and the clock records,
he remains, mentally, a boy.

There was the fate of a whole generation: indeed, is it not
still the fate of perhaps the great majority of Americans, lost
in their dreams of a great fortune in real-estate, rubber, or oil?
In our heroic moments, we may think of ourselves as Leather-
stockings, or two-fisted fellows like Paul Bunyan; but in the
bottom of our hearts, we are disconsolate Rips. In this process
of uneasy transition, in the endless experimentalism and externality of the American scheme, the American came to feel
that something was wrong. He saw no way of rectifying the
fact itself; the necessity to be "up and moving" seemed written
in the skies. In his disappointment and frustration, he became
maudlin. It is no accident that our most sentimental popular
songs all date back to the earlier half of the Nineteenth Century. At the moment when the eagle screamed loudest, when
the words Manifest Destiny were put into circulation, when

Colonel Diver, the fire-eater, Jefferson Brick, the editor of the Rowdy Journal, and Scadder, the real-estate gambler, were joining voices in a Hallelujah of triumph,—it was then that the tear of regret and the melancholy clutch of the Adam's apple made their way into the ballad.

The great song of the mid-century was "Don't you remember Sweet Alice, Ben Bolt?" but the truth is that Alice was merely a name to start the tears rolling. It was not over the fate of Alice that the manly heart grieved: what hurt was the fact that in the short space of twenty years, the mill-wheel had fallen to pieces, the rafters had tumbled in, the cabin had gone to ruin, the tree had been felled, and "where once the lord of the forest waved" were grass and golden grain. In short, ruin and change lay in the wake of the pioneer, as he went westering. "There is change in the things I loved, Ben Bolt, they have changed from the old to the new," and somehow this progressive generation had an uneasy suspicion that they were not changing altogether for the better. What a conflict was in the pioneer's bosom! He pulls up stakes, to the tune of Home Sweet Home. He sells his parcel of real estate to the next gambler who will hold it, still sighing "there is no place like home." He guts out the forest: "Woodman, spare that tree, touch not a single bough, in youth it sheltered me, and I'll protect it now." And in the struggle of scalping one of the Red Varmints he is driving to the Land of the Sunset the Song of Hiawatha slips from his hip-pocket.

Does this seem to exaggerate the conflict? Be assured that it was there. The Mark Twains, Bret Hartes, and Artemus Wards would not have found the old solidities of Europe so ingratiating, taught as they were to despise Europe's cities and institutions as the relics of a miserable and feudal past, if the life they had known had not too often starved their essential humanity.

IV

With the experience of the Great War behind us, we can now understand a little better the psychal state of our various American communities, whilst they were immersed in their besetting "war against Nature." A war automatically either draws people into the service, or, if they resist, unfits them for carrying on their civil duties in a whole-hearted manner. In the pioneer's war against Nature, every member of the community was bound to take part, or be branded as a dilettante, a skulker, a deserter. The phrases that were used in justification of pioneering during the Nineteenth Century were not those which set the Romantic Movement in action in the Eighteenth: these newcomers sought to "conquer a wilderness," "subdue Nature," "take possession of the continent." "To act that each to-morrow finds us *farther* than to-day," was the very breath of the new pioneer mores: the Psalm of Life was the sum of the pioneer's life.

The throb and urge of this grand march across the continent communicated itself to those who remained in the East. The non-combatants in Boston, Philadelphia, and New York were as uneasy and hesitating in their activities as a conscript who expects at any moment to be called to the colors. Some of them, like C. F. Adams, were only too happy when the Civil War turned the call of the pioneer into a command; others, like George Perkins Marsh confessed that "in our place and day the scholar hath no vocation," and made plain with what reluctance they turned their backs upon science and the humane arts to struggle in the world of business; others, like William Cullen Bryant, threw a handful of Nature poems into the scales, to weigh over against a life of zealous energy in newspaperdom. In these, and many other equally irritating biographies, one finds that the myth of the Pioneer Conquest had taken possession of even the finer and more sensitive minds: they accepted the uglinesses and brutalities of pioneering, even as many of our contemporaries accepted the bestialities of war, and instead of recognizing no other necessity than their best desires, they throttled their desires and bowed to an imaginary necessity. In the end, the pioneer was as far from Rousseau and Wordsworth as the inventor of poison gas was from the troubadour who sang the Song of Roland.

The effect of the pioneer habits upon our culture has become a commonplace of literary criticism during the last half-generation; the weakness of this criticism has been the failure to grasp the difference in origin between the puritan, the pioneer, and the inventor-business man. The Puritan did indeed pave the way for the extroverts that came after him; but what he really sought was an inner grace. The pioneer debased all the old values of a settled culture, and made the path of a dehumanized industrialism in America as smooth as a concrete road; but it was only in the habits he had developed, so to say, on the road, that he turned aside from the proper goal of the Romantic Movement, which was to find a basis for a fresh effort in culture, and gave himself over to the inventor-businessman's search for power. All three, Puritan, pioneer, and businessman came to exist through the breakdown of Europe's earlier, integrated culture; but, given the wide elbow room of America, each type tended to develop to its extreme, only to emerge in succeeding generations into the composite character of that fictitious person, the Average American.

In order to appreciate the distance between the America of the Eighteenth Century, which was still attached umbilically to the older Europe, and the America of the pioneer, tinctured by the puritan and the industrialist, one might perhaps compare two representative men, Thomas Jefferson and Mark Twain. When Mark Twain went to Europe during the Gilded Age, he was really an innocent abroad: his experience in Roughing It had not fitted him for any sort of seasoned contact with climates, councils, governments. When Jefferson went to Paris from the backwoods of Virginia, a hundred years earlier, he was a cultivated man, walking among his peers: he criticized English architecture, not as Mark Twain might have done, because it was effete and feudal, but because it was even more barbarous than that of the American provinces. To Mark Twain, as to most of his contemporaries, industry appeared in the light of what sporting people call a good thing; when, after sinking a small fortune in a new typesetting machine, he approached his friend H. H. Rogers with another invention, the chief attraction he emphasized was its potential monopoly. Jefferson's concern with the practical arts, on the other hand, was personal and esthetic: he was an active farmer, with a carefully

kept nursery book, and he brought back to America prints and
measurements of public buildings, which served him in the design of his own.

The death of Jefferson, the scholar, the artist, the statesman,
and agriculturist—one of the last true figures of the Renaissance—was symbolic; for it came in 1826, just at the moment
when the great westward expansion began. In two men of the
following generation, S. F. B. Morse and Edgar Allan Poe, we
find the new pioneer mores working towards their two legitimate goals. Morse defended his preoccupation with criticism,
instead of painting, in words that might have been framed as
an illustration of the mood I have been trying to describe. "If
I am to be the Pioneer, and am fitted for it, why should I not
glory as much in felling trees and clearing away rubbish as in
showing the decorations suited to a more advanced state of culture?" As for Poe, the Walpole of a belated Gothic revival, he
recorded in literature the displacement and dissociation that
was taking place in the community's life.

With no conscious connection with the life about him, Poe
became nevertheless the literary equivalent of the industrialist
and the pioneer. I have no desire to speak lightly of Poe's capacities as a critic of literature, which were high, nor of his
skill in the formal exercises of literary composition. Poe was
the first artist consciously to give the short-story a succinct and
final form; and as an esthetic experimentalist his own arrangements in prose prepared the way, among other things, for Bau-
delaire's prose poems. Yet Poe's meticulous and rationalistic
mind fitted his environment and mirrored its inner characteristics far more readily than a superficial look at it would lead
one to believe. In him, the springs of human desire had not
so much frozen up as turned to metal: his world was, in one
of his favorite words, plutonian, like that of Watt and Fulton
and Gradgrind: the tears that he dropped were steel beads, and
his mind worked like a mechanical hopper, even when there
were no appropriate materials to throw into it. It happened to
be a very good mind; and when it had something valuable to
work upon, as in literary criticism, the results were often excellent. Left to himself, however, he either spent his energies on

small ingenuities like ciphers and "scientific" puzzles, or he created a synthetic world, half-pasteboard and half-perfume, whose
thinness as an imaginative reality was equaled only by its apparent dissociation from the actualities that surrounded him.
The criticism of Poe's fantasies is not that they were "unreal":
Shakespeare's are equally so: the criticism is that they have
their sources in a starved and limited humanity, the same
starved and limited humanity in which Gradgrind devoted himself to "hard facts," and the frontier fighter to cold steel. Terror and cruelty dominated Poe's mind; and terror and cruelty
leave a scar on almost every tale and anecdote about pioneer
life.

The emotional equivalence of Poe's fiction and the pioneer's
fact was perhaps a matter of chance; I will not strain my point
by trying to make out a case for anything else. That the equivalence is not a meretricious presumption on my part, is attested,
I think, by the fact that it was corroborated a generation later
in the anecdotes of Mark Twain and the short stories of
Ambrose Bierce. No sensitive mind can undergo warfare or
pioneering, with all the raw savagery of human nature developed to the full, without undergoing a shock. The massacres,
the banditries, even the coarse practical jokes, all left their de-
testable impressions. There is a mock-sinister side to the Romantic Movement in European literature in the horror stories
of Walpole and Mrs. Radcliffe; but these stories are mere pap
for infants alongside those Mark Twain was able to recount in
almost every chapter of Roughing It and Life on the Mississippi.

Poe, perhaps, had never heard one of these stories; but the
dehumanized world he created gave a place for terrors, cruel-
ties, and murders which expressed, in a sublimated and eminently readable form, the sadisms and masochisms of the pioneer's life. Man is, after all, a domestic animal; and though
he may return to unbroken nature as a relief from all the so-
brieties of existence, he can reside for long in the wilderness
only by losing some of the essential qualities of the cultivated
human species. Poe had lost these qualities, neurotically, without even seeing the wilderness. Cooper's generation had

dreamed of Leatherstocking; in realization, the dream had become the nightmare world of Poe. There is scarcely a page of reliable testimony about pioneer life which does not hint at this nightmare. The testimony is all the more salient when one finds Mark Twain reciting his horrors in a vein of pure innocence, without a word of criticism, and then, by a psychic transfer, becoming ferociously indignant over the same things when he finds them in his imaginary Court of King Arthur.

v

The vast gap between the hope of the Romantic Movement and the reality of the pioneer period is one of the most sardonic jests of history. On one side, the bucolic innocence of the Eighteenth Century, its belief in a fresh start, and its attempt to achieve a new culture. And over against it, the epic march of the covered wagon, leaving behind it deserted villages, bleak cities, depleted soils, and the sick and exhausted souls that engraved their epitaphs in Mr. Masters' Spoon River Anthology. Against the genuine heroism and derring-do that accompanied this movement, and against the real gains that it achieved here and there in the spread of social well-being, must be set off the crudities of the pioneer's sexual life, his bestial swilling and drinking and bullying, and his barbarities in dealing with the original inhabitants—"a fierce dull biped standing in our way." The gun and the ax and the pick, alas! had taught their lessons only too well; and the more social and co-operative groups, like the Mormons, were attacked violently, but always under the cover of high moral indignation, by belligerent worthies whose morals would have given a bad odor to a hangman's picnic.

The truth is that the life of the pioneer was bare and insufficient: he did not really face Nature, he merely evaded society. Divorced from its social context, his experience became meaningless. That is why, perhaps, he kept on changing his occupation and his habitat, for as long as he could keep on moving he could forget that, in his own phrase, he was not "getting anywhere." He had no end of experiences: he could shoot, build, plant, chop, saw, dicker: he was Ulysses, Nimrod,

Noah, and Cain all bundled into one man. But there was, all too literally, no end to these activities—that is, no opportunity to refine them, to separate the ore from the slag, to live them over again in the mind. In short, the pioneer experience did not produce a rounded pioneer culture; and if the new settler began as an unconscious follower of Rousseau, he was only too ready, after the first flush of effort, to barter all his glorious heritage for gas light and paved streets and starched collars and skyscrapers and the other insignia of a truly high and progressive civilization. The return to Nature led, ironically, to a denatured environment, and when, after the long journey was over, the pioneer became conscious once more of the social obligation, these interests manifested themselves in covert pathological ways, like campaigns to prohibit the cigarette or to prescribe the length of sheets for hotel beds, or to promote institutions of compulsory good fellowship. So much for an experience that failed either to absorb an old culture or create a new one!

Chapter Three The Golden Day

THE MORNING STAR

I

No one who was awake in the early part of the Nineteenth Century was unaware that in the practical arrangements of life men were on the brink of a great change. The rumble of the industrial revolution was heard in the distance long before the storm actually broke; and before American society was completely transformed through the work of the land-pioneer and the industrial pioneer, there arose here and there over the land groups of people who anticipated the effects of this revolution and were in revolt against all its preoccupations. Some of these groups reverted to an archaic theocracy, like that of the Mormons, in which a grotesque body of beliefs was combined with an extraordinary amount of economic sagacity and statesmanship; some of them became disciples of Fourier and sought to live in coöperative colonies, which would foster men's various capacities more fully than the utilitarian community.

The air quivered with both hope and trepidation. In the new industrial cities, the slum made its appearance; great bodies of depauperate immigrants with strange traditions altered the balance of power; politics became the business of clever rapscallions who looted the public treasury; by the end of the fifties an editorial writer in Harper's Weekly prayed for professional administrators who might bring a public conscience into the corrupt democracy of the big cities. In general, all the forces that blighted America after the Civil War existed in embryonic form between 1830 and 1860. At the same time, the older regions began to reap the fruits of two centuries of contact with the new soil and new customs. It is at the hour when the old ways are breaking up that men step outside them sufficiently to feel their beauty and significance: lovers are often closest at the moment of parting. In New England, the inherited medieval civilization had become a shell; but, drying up, it left behind a sweet acrid aroma, and for a brief day it had a more intense existence in the spirit. Before the life itself collapsed, men felt the full weight of it in their imagination. In the act of passing away, the Puritan begot the Transcendentalist, and the will-to-power, which had made him what he was, with his firm but forbidding character, and his conscientious but narrow activity, gave way to the will-to-perfection.

The period from 1830 to 1860 was in America one of disintegration and fulfillment: the new and the old, the crude and the complete, the base and the noble mingled together. Puritan fanatics like Goodyear brought to the vulcanization of rubber the same intense passion that Thoreau brought to Nature: sharp mountebanks like Barnum grew out of the same sort of Connecticut village that nourished an inspired schoolmaster like Bronson Alcott: genuine statesmen like Brigham Young organized the colonization of Utah whilst nonentities like Pierce and Buchanan governed the whole country. During this period, the old culture of the seaboard settlement had its Golden Day in the mind; the America of the migrations, on the other hand, partly because of weaknesses developed in the pioneer, partly because of the one-sided interests of the industrialist, and partly because of the volcanic eruption of the Civil War had up to 1890 little more than the boomtown optimism of the Gilded Age to justify its existence.

Despite the foreboding that every intelligent mind felt when it contemplated the barbarism of the industrial age, inimical to any culture except that which grew out of its own inhuman absorption in abstract matter and abstract power, the dominant note of the period was one of hope. Before the Civil War the promise of the Westward march expanded the sense of achievement that came over the Eastern States; and men faced the world with a confidence that went beyond the complacent optimism of the British Utilitarians—tainted as that was by Carlyle's dire reminders of the palpable wreckage and jetsam that had been washed into the slums of London, Manchester, and Birmingham on the wave of "industrial prosperity."

There were no Carlyles or Ruskins in America during this period; they were almost unthinkable. One might live in this atmosphere, or one might grapple with the White Whale and die; but if one lived, one lived without distrust, without inner complaint, and even if one scorned the ways of one's fellows, as Thoreau did, one remained among them, and sought to remedy in oneself the abuses that existed in society. Transcendentalism might criticize a fossilized past; but no one imagined that the future could be equally fossilized. The testimony is unqualified. One breathed hope, as one might breathe the heady air of early autumn, pungent with the smell of hickory fires and baking bread, as one walked through the village street.

"One cannot look on the freedom of this country, in connection with its youth," wrote Emerson in The Young American, "without a presentment that here shall laws and institutions exist in some proportion to the majesty of Nature. . . . It is a country of beginnings, of projects, of vast designs and expectations. It has no past: all has an onward and prospective look." The voice of Whitman echoed Emerson through a trumpet: but that of Melville, writing in 1850, was no less sanguine and full-pulsed: "God has predestinated, mankind expects, great things from our race; and great things we feel in our souls. The rest of the nations must soon be in our rear. We are the pioneers of the world; the advance guard, sent on through the wilderness of untried things, to break a new path in the New World that is ours. In our youth is our strength; in our inexperience, our wisdom."

"Every institution is the lengthened shadow of a man." Here and there in America during its Golden Day grew up a man who cast a shadow over the landscape. They left no labor-saving machines, no discoveries, and no wealthy bequests to found a library or a hospital: what they left was something much less and much more than that—an heroic conception of life. They peopled the landscape with their own shapes. This period nourished men, as no other has done in America before or since. Up to that time, the American communities were provincial; when it was over, they had lost their base, and spreading all over the landscape, deluged with newcomers speaking strange languages and carrying on Old-World customs, they lost that essential likeness which is a necessary basis for intimate communication. The first settlement was complete: agricultural and industrial life were still in balance in the older parts of the country; and on the seas trade opened up activities for the adventurous. When Ticknor was preparing to go to Germany, in the first decade of the century, there was but one German dictionary, apparently, in New England. Within a generation, Goethe was translated, selections from the European classics were published; and importations of the Indian, Chinese and Persian classics widened the horizon of people who had known India only by its shawls, China only by its tea.

The traffic of the American merchantman across the seas brought ideas with every load of goods. Living lustily in all these new experiences, the pushing back of the frontier, the intercourse with the Ancient East, the promises of science and invention—steamboats: railroads: telegraphs: rubber raincoats: reapers: Von Baer: Faraday: Darwin:—living in these things, and believing in them, the capacity for philosophic exploration increased, too; and when an Emerson went into retreat, he retired with an armful of experiences and ideas comparable only to the treasuries that the Elizabethans grandly looted. Within the circle of the daily fact, the Transcendentalists might protest against the dull materialism which was beginning to dominate the period: but it needed only a little boldness to convert the materialism itself into a source of new potencies.

An imaginative New World came to birth during this period, a new hemisphere in the geography of the mind. That world was the climax of American experience. What preceded led up to it: what followed, dwindled away from it; and we who think and write to-day are either continuing the first exploration, or we are disheartened, and relapse into some stale formula, or console ourselves with empty gestures of frivolity.

The American scene was a challenge; and men rose to it. The writers of this period were not alone; if they were outcasts in the company of the usual run of merchants, manufacturers, and politicians, they were at all events attended by a company of people who had shared their experience and moved on eagerly with it. When all is reckoned, however, there is nothing in the minor writers that is not pretty fully recorded by Emerson, Thoreau, Whitman, Melville, and Hawthorne. These men, as Mr. D. H. Lawrence has well said, reached a verge. They stood between two worlds. Part of their experience enabled them to bring the protestant movement to its conclusion: the critical examination of men, creeds, and institutions, which is the vital core of protestantism, could not go much further. But already, out of another part of their experience, that which arose out of free institutions planted in an unpreëmpted soil, molded by fresh contact with forest and sea and the more ingenious works of man, already this experience pushed them beyond the pit Melville fell into, and led them towards new institutions, a new art, a new philosophy, formed on the basis of a wider past than the European, caught by his Mediterranean or Palestinian cultures, was capable of seizing.

It was the organic break with Europe's past that enabled the American to go on; just as the immigration of people to America came to include specimens from almost all the folk of the world, so the American past widened sufficiently to bring Eastern and Western cultures into a common focus. The American went on. Whereas, in their search for a new basis for culture, Nietzsche went back to pre-Socratic Greece, Carlyle to Abbot Samson, Tolstoi and Dostoevsky to primitive Christianity, and Wagner to the early Germanic fables, Emerson, Thoreau, and Whitman went forward leaning on the experiences about them, using the past as the logger uses the corduroy road, to push further into the wilderness and still have a sound bottom under him. They fathomed the possibilities, these Americans, of a modern basis for culture, and fathoming it, were nearer to the sources of culture, nearer to the formative thinkers and poets of the past, than those who sought to restore the past. What is vital in the American writers of the Golden Day grew out of a life which opened up to them every part of their social heritage. And a thousand more experiences and fifty million more people have made us no wiser. The spiritual fact remains unalterable, as Emerson said, by many or few particulars. It is the spiritual fact of American experience that we shall examine during the period of its clearest expression.

II

All the important thinkers who shared in this large experience were born between 1800 and 1820; their best work was done by the time the Civil War came; if not beyond the reach of its hurt, they at all events could not be completely overthrown or warped by it. The leader of these minds, the central figure of them all, was Ralph Waldo Emerson. He was the first American philosopher with a fresh doctrine: he was the first American poet with a fresh theme: he was the first American prose writer to escape, by way of the Elizabethan dramatists and the Seventeenth Century preachers, from the smooth prose of Addison or the stilted periods of Johnson. He was an original, in the sense that he was a source: he was the glacier that became the white mountain torrent of Thoreau, and expanded into the serene, ample-bosomed lake of Whitman. He loses a little by this icy centrality: he must be climbed, and there is so much of him that people become satisfied with a brief glimpse, and forget that they have not reached the summit which dominates the lower peaks and platforms. His very coldness seems familiar to academic minds; and for too long they appropriated him, as one of them: they forgot that his coldness is not that of an impotence, but of an inner intensity: it burns! The outward manner of his life was mild: there are summer afternoons when from the distance Mont Blanc itself seems little more than a cone of ice-cream; and his contemporaries forgot that this sweet man carried a lash, a lash that would not merely drive the money-changers from the temple but the priests.

Emerson was a sort of living essence. The preacher, the farmer, the scholar, the sturdy New England freeholder, yes, and the shrewd Yankee peddler or mechanic, were all encompassed by him; but what they meant in actual life had fallen away from him: he represented what they stood for in eternity. With Emerson's works one might reconstruct the landscape and society of New England: a few things would be left out from Nature which Thoreau would have to supply for us—a handful of flora and fauna, and the new Irish immigrants who were already building the railroads and who finally were to take possession of Boston—but what remained would still be everything of importance in the New England scheme of things. The weaknesses of New England are there, too: its bookishness, its failure, as Margaret Fuller said of Emerson, to kiss the earth sufficiently, its impatience to assume too quickly an upright position, its too-tidy moral housekeeping. Strong or weak, Emerson was complete: in his thought the potentialities of New England were finally expressed.

It is almost impossible to sum up Emerson's doctrine, for he touched life on many sides, and what is more, he touched it freshly, so though he is a Platonist, one will not find Plato's doctrines of Art in his essay on Art; and though he was in a very derivative way a Kantian, one will not find Kant's principles at the bottom of his ethics. With most of the resources of the past at his command, Emerson achieved nakedness: his central doctrine is the virtue of this intellectual, or cultural, nakedness: the virtue of getting beyond the institution, the habit, the ritual, and finding out what it means afresh in one's own consciousness. Protestantism had dared to go this far with respect to certain minor aspects of the Catholic cult: Emerson applied the same method in a more sweeping way, and buoyed up by his faith in the future of America—a country endowed with perhaps every advantage except venerability—he asked not merely what Catholic ritual means, but all ritual, not merely what dynastic politics means but all politics; and so with every other important aspect of life. Emerson divested everything of its associations, and seized it afresh, to make what associations it could with the life he had lived and the experience he had assimilated. As a result, each part of the past came to him on equal terms: Buddha had perhaps as much to give as Christ: Hafiz could teach him as much as Shakespeare or Dante. Moreover, every fragment of present experience lost its associated values, too: towards the established hierarchy of experiences, with vested interests that no longer, perhaps, could exhibit the original power of sword or spade, he extended the democratic challenge: perhaps new ex-

periences belonged to the summit of aristocracy, and old lines
were dying out, or were already dead, leaving only empty ven-
erated names.

Emerson saw the implications of this attempt to re-think life,
and to accept only what was his. He did not shrink from them.
"Nothing is at last sacred but the integrity of your own mind.
. . . I remember an answer which when quite young I was
prompted to make to a valued adviser, who was wont to impor-
tune me with the dear old doctrines of the church. On my saying, 'What have I to do with the sacredness of traditions, if I live
wholly from within?' my friend suggested,—'But these impulses
may be from below, not from above.' I replied, 'They do not
seem to me to be such; but if I am the Devil's child, I will live
then from the Devil.' No law can be sacred to me but that of
my Nature."

"Life only avails, not the having lived." There is the kernel
of the Emersonian doctrine of self-reliance: it is the answer
which the American, in the day of his confidence and achievement, flung back into the face of Europe, where the "having
lived" has always been so conspicuous and formidable. In a certain sense, this doctrine was a barbarism; but it was a creative
barbarism, a barbarism that aimed to use the old buildings not
as a shell, but as a quarry; neither casting them aside altogether, nor attempting wretchedly to fit a new and lush existence
into the old forms. The transcendental young photographer,
in Hawthorne's House of the Seven Gables, suggested that
houses should be built afresh every generation, instead of lingering on in dingy security, never really fitting the needs of any
family, but that which originally conceived and built it. An un-
creative age is aghast at this suggestion: for the new building
may be cruder than the old, the new problem may not awaken
sufficient creative capacities, equal to the previous one: these
are the necessary counsels of prudence, impotence.

In the heyday of the American adventure, neither Emerson
nor Hawthorne was afraid. Emerson re-thought life, and in the
mind he coined new shapes and images and institutions, ready
to take the place of those he discarded. A building was perish-
able; a custom might fall into disuse; but what of it? The mind

was inexhaustible; and it was only the unawakened and un-
imaginative practical people who did not feel that these dearly
purchased trinkets might all be thrown into the melting pot and
shaped over again, without a penny lost. It was not that nakedness itself was so desirable: but clothes were cheap! Why keep
on piecing together and patching the old doctrines, when the
supply never could run out, so long as life nourished Emersons?
"We shall not always set so great a price," he exclaimed, "on a
few texts, a few lives. We are like children who repeat by rote
the sentences of grandames and tutors, and, as they grow older,
of the men of talents and character they chance to see,—painfully recollecting the exact words they spoke; afterwards, when
they come into the point of view which these had who uttered
these sayings, they understand them, and are willing to let the
words go; for at any time, they can use words as good when the
occasion comes. . . . When we have new perceptions, we shall
gladly disburden the memory of its hoarded treasures, as of old
rubbish."

III

The Platonism of Emerson's mind has been overemphasized;
or rather, it has been misconstrued to mean that he lived in
a perpetual cloud-world. The truth is, however, that Emerson's
Platonism was not a matter simply of following Plato: it was a
matter of living like Plato, and achieving a similar mode of
thought. Critics have too often spoken of Plato's forms as if they
were merely a weak escape from the urgent problems of Fifth-
Century Athens; and of Emerson's, as if they were a neurotic
withdrawal from the hurly-burly of American life. They were
both, in a sense, a withdrawal; but it was a withdrawal of water
into a reservoir, or of grain into a bin, so that they might be
available later, if they could not be effectively distributed at
once. Both Plato and Emerson had mixed with the life about
them and knew its concrete details: both were conscious of the
purely makeshift character of existing institutions; both were
aware that they were in a period of transition. Instead of busy-
ing himself with the little details of political or economic read-
justment, each sought to achieve a pattern which would permit

the details to fall into place, and so make possible a creative renovation. Emerson wrote about Man the Reformer; but he never belonged to any political sect or cult. The blight of Negro slavery awakened his honest anger, and his essay on the Know-nothings is an excellent diatribe: but even this great issue did not cause him to lose his perspective: he sought to abolish the white slaves who maintained that institution.

In coupling Emerson's name with Plato's I have hinted that Emerson was a philosopher; I see no reason to qualify this hint, or to apologize for the juxtaposition. He has been more or less grudgingly given such a place by current philosophic commentators, because on a superficial examination there is no originality in his metaphysics: both Plato and Kant had given an independent reality to the world of ideas, and the habit of treating existing facts as symbols is so ancient it became a shocking novelty when reëmployed in our own time by Dr. Sigmund Freud. The bare metaphysical outlines of Emerson's work give no insight, however, into the body of his thought as a whole. The contents of Emerson's philosophy is much richer, I think, than that of any of his contemporaries; and he is denied a high place in philosophy largely because the content is so rich that it cannot be recognized, in the attentuated twilight of academic groves, as philosophy. Hegel and Comte and Spencer, Emerson's contemporaries, had all found formulæ which led them into relations with a vast mass of concrete facts: the weakness of their several philosophies was due to severe defects of personality—they were sexually neurotic, like Comte, with his pathetic apotheosis of Clothilde, or they were querulous invalids, like Spencer, who had never been able to correct by a wider experience the original bias given to his mind by his early training as a railroad engineer. Emerson had the good fortune to live a healthy and symmetrical life: he answered Tolstoi's demand for essential greatness—he had no kinks. In him, philosophy resumed the full gamut of human experience it had known in Pythagoras and Plato.

Emerson's uniqueness, for his time, consists in the fact that he appreciated not merely the factual data of science, and the instrumental truth of scientific investigation: he also recognized the formative rôle of ideas, and he saw the importance of "dia-lectic" in placing new patterns before the mind which did not exist, ready-made, in the order of Nature. "All the facts of the animal economy, sex, nutriment, gestation, birth, growth, are symbols of the passage of the world into the soul of man, to suf-fer there a change, and reappear a new and higher fact." The occasion for, or the efficacy of, this passage into the soul of man was denied by the externalism of Nineteenth Century empiri-cism; obscurely, it was the ground for contention between reli-gion and science, a quarrel which religion lost by holding fast to a purely superstitious empiricism. If instrumental truths are the only order of truth, all religion is a superstition, all poetry a puerility, and all art itself is a weak anticipation of photogra-phy and mechanical drawing.

Emerson's affirmation of both physics and dialectic, of both science and myth, an affirmation which justified the existence of the artist, the poet, the saint, was of prime importance; for he did not make the mistake of disdaining the order and power that science had achieved within its proper department. Emer-son was a Darwinist before the Origin of Species was published, because he was familiar with the investigations which were link-ing together the chain of organic continuity, and he was ready to follow the facts wherever they would lead him. Agassiz, Cam-bridge's great man of science, accepted the facts, too; but he was afraid of them; insulated in his evangelical Christianity, he in-sisted that the facts did not exist in Nature but in the mind of God. Emerson was untroubled by Agassiz's reluctance: the func-tion of "God" was perpetually being performed for him in the passage of the world into the soul of man; and there was noth-ing in his philosophy to make him deny an orderly sequence in Nature. For Emerson, matter and spirit were not enemies in conflict: they were phases of man's experience: matter passed into spirit and became a symbol: spirit passed into matter and gave it a form; and symbols and forms were the essences through which man lived and fulfilled his proper being. Who was there among Emerson's contemporaries in the Nineteenth Century that was gifted with such a complete vision? To withhold the name of philosopher from the man who saw and expressed this integral vision of life so clearly is to deny the central office of philosophy.

Emerson's thought does not seal the world up into a few packets, tied with a formula, and place them in a pigeonhole. In the past, it was not limited to a phase of Christianity, nor a phase of classic culture: it roamed over a much wider area, and as he himself suggested, used Plato and Proclus, not for what they were, but as so many added colors for his palette. The past for Emerson was neither a prescription nor a burden: it was rather an esthetic experience. Being no longer inevitable in America, that is, no longer something handed down with a fellowship at Oxford or a place at court, the past could be entertained freely and experimentally. It could be revalued; and the paradox of Brahma became as acceptable as the paradox that the meek shall inherit the earth.

The poet, for Emerson, was the liberator; and in that sense, he was a great poet. With him one does not feel that our "civilization nears its meridian, but rather that we are yet only at the cock-crowing and the morning star." The promise of America, of an unspotted Nature and a fresh start, had seeped into every pore of Emerson's mind. "Do not set the least value on what I do," he warns, "nor the least discredit on what I do not, as if I pretended to settle anything as true or false. I unsettle all things. No facts to me are sacred; none are profane; I simply experiment, an endless seeker, with no Past at my back. . . . Why should we import rags and relics into the new hour? . . . Nothing is secure but life, transition, the energizing spirit. No love can be bound by oath or covenant to secure it against a higher love. No truth so sublime but it may be trivial tomorrow in the light of new thoughts. People wish to be settled: only as far as they are unsettled is there any hope for them."

The vigor of this challenge, the challenge of the American wilderness, the challenge of the new American society, where the European lost the security of his past in order to gain a better stake in the future—who but can feel that this is what was distinguished and interesting in our American experience, and

what was salutary, for all its incidental defects, in the dumb
physical bravado of the pioneer? Two men met the challenge
and carried it further: Thoreau and Whitman. They completed
the Emersonian circle, carrying the potted flower of the scholar's
study out into the spring sunshine, the upturned earth, and the
keen air.

THE DAWN

IV

THE pioneer who broke the trail westward left scarcely a trace
of his adventure in the mind: what remains are the tags of pioneer customs, and mere souvenirs of the past, like the Pittsburg
stogy, which is our living connection to-day with the Conestoga
wagon, whose drivers used to roll cigars as the first covered wag-
ons plodded over the Alleghenies.

What the pioneer felt, if he felt anything, in the midst of
these new solitudes; what he dreamt, if he dreamt anything; all
these things we must surmise from a few snatches of song, from
the commonplace reports issued as the trail was nearing its end,
by the generation of Mark Twain and Hamlin Garland, or by
the reflections of their sons and daughters, romantically eager,
like John G. Neihardt's, critically reflective, like Susan Glaspell's, or wistfully sordid, like Edgar Lee Masters' Anthology.
Those who really faced the wilderness, and sought to make
something out of it, remained in the East; in their reflection,
one sees the reality that might have been. Henry David Thoreau was perhaps the only man who paused to give a report of
the full experience. In a period when men were on the move,
he remained still; when men were on the make, he remained
poor; when civil disobedience broke out in the lawlessness of
the cattle thief and the mining town rowdy, by sheer neglect,
Thoreau practiced civil disobedience as a principle, in protest
against the Mexican War, the Fugitive Slave Law, and slavery
itself. Thoreau in his life and letters shows what the pioneer
movement might have come to if this great migration had
sought culture rather than material conquest, and an intensity
of life, rather than mere extension over the continent.

Born in Concord about half a generation after Emerson, Thoreau found himself without the preliminary searchings and reachings of the young clergyman. He started from the point that his fellow-townsman, Emerson, had reached; and where the first cleared out of his mind every idea that made no direct connections with his personal experience, Thoreau cleared out of his life itself every custom or physical apparatus, to boot, which could not stand up and justify its existence. "A native of the United States," De Tocqueville had observed, "clings to the world's goods as if he were certain never to die; and he is so hasty at grasping at all within his reach, that one would suppose he was constantly afraid of not living long enough to enjoy them. He clutches everything, he holds nothing fast, but soon loosens his grasp to pursue fresh gratifications." Thoreau completely reversed this process: it was because he wanted to live fully that he turned away from everything that did not serve towards this end. He prized the minutes for what they brought, and would not exercise his citizenship at the town meeting, if a spring day by Walden Pond had greater promise; nor would he fill his hours with gainful practices, as a maker of pencils or a surveyor, beyond what was needed for the bare business of keeping his bodily self warm and active.

Thoreau seized the opportunity to consider what in its essentials a truly human life was; he sought, in Walden, to find out what degree of food, clothing, shelter, labor was necessary to sustain it. It was not animal hardihood or a merely tough physical regimen he was after; nor did he fancy, for all that he wrote in contempt of current civilization, that the condition of the woodcutter, the hunter, or the American Indian was in itself to be preferred. What he discovered was that people are so eager to get the ostentatious "necessaries" of a civil life that they lose the opportunity to profit by civilization itself: while their physical wants are complicated, their lives, culturally, are not enriched in proportion, but are rather pauperized and bleached.

Thoreau was completely oblivious to the dominant myths that had been bequeathed by the Seventeenth Century. Indifferent to the illusion of magnitude, he felt that Walden Pond, rightly viewed, was as vast as the ocean, and the woods and fields and swamps of Concord were as inexhaustible as the Dark Continent. In his study of Nature, he had recourse on occasion to the scientific botanists and zoölogists; but he himself had possession of a method that they were slow to arrive at; and it is easier for us to-day to understand the metaphysical distinction of Thoreau's kind of nature study than it would have been for Gray or Agassiz. Like Wordsworth before him, like Bergson after him, he realized that in current science "we murder to dissect," and he passed beyond the artful dismemberments of contemporary science to the flower and the bird and the habitat themselves. "Not a single scientific term or distinction," he wrote once in his notebook, "is the least to the purpose. You would fain perceive something and you must approach the object totally unprejudiced. You must be aware that nothing is what you take it to be. . . . Your greatest success will be simply to perceive that such things are, and you will have no communication to make to the Royal Society." In other words, Thoreau sought in nature all the manifold qualities of being; he was not merely in search of those likenesses or distinctions which help to create classified indexes and build up a system. The esthetic qualities of a fern were as important for his mode of apprehension as the number of spores on a frond; it was not that he disdained science, but that, like the old herbalists and naturalists he admired, he would not let the practical offices of science, its classification, its measurements, its numerations, take precedence over other forms of understanding. Science, practiced in this fashion, is truly part of a humane life, and a Darwin dancing for joy over a slide in his microscope, or a Pupin, finding the path to physics through his contemplation of the stars he watched as a herd-boy through the night, are not poorer scientists but richer ones for these joys and delights: they merely bow to the bias of utilitarianism when they leave these things out of their reports. In his attitude toward scientific truth Thoreau was perhaps a prophetic figure; and a new age may do honor to his metaphysics as well as to his humanity.

The resolute acceptance of his immediate milieu as equal to the utmost that the earth could offer stood by Thoreau in his other activities, too. He captained huckleberry parties as he might have led a battle, and was just as much the leader in one as he would have been in the other. His courage he reserved for better occasions than the battlefield, for he was ready to go to jail for his principles, and to mock Emerson for remaining outside. As for his country, he loved the land too well to confuse it with the shifting territorial boundaries of the National State. In this, he had that vital regional consciousness which every New Englander shared: Hawthorne himself had said that New England was as large a piece of territory as could claim his allegiance. Thoreau was not deceived by the rascality of politicians, who were ready to wage war for a coveted patch of Mexico's land; nor did he side with those who, for the sake of the Union, were ready to give up the principles that alone had made the Union valuable. What he loved was the landscape, his friends, and his companions in the spirit: when the Political State presumed to exercise a brass counter-claim on these loyalties it might go to the devil.

Thoreau's attitude toward the State, one must note, was just the opposite to that of the progressive pioneer. The latter did not care what sort of landscape he "located" in, so long as he could salute the flag of his country and cast his vote: Thoreau, on the contrary, was far too religious a man to commit the idolatry of saluting a symbol of secular power; and he realized that the affairs controlled by the vote represented only a small fraction of an interesting life, while so far from being indifferent to the land itself, he absorbed it, as men have absorbed legends, and guarded it, as men preserve ceremonies. The things which his contemporaries took for the supreme realities of life, matter, money, and political rights, had only an instrumental use for Thoreau: they might contribute a little to the arrangement of a good life, but the good life itself was not contained, was not even implied in them. One might spend one's life pursuing them without having lived. "There is not one of my readers," he exclaimed, "who has yet lived a whole human life."

In Thoreau's time, industrialism had begun to puff itself up over its multiplication of goods and the increase of wants that it fostered, in order to provide the machine with an outlet for its ever-too-plentiful supply. Thoreau simply asked: "Shall we always study to obtain more of these things, and not sometimes be content with less?" "If we do not get our sleepers and forge rails and devote long days and nights to work," he observed ironically, "but go tinkering with our lives to improve *them*, who will build the railroads?" Thoreau was not a penurious fanatic, who sought to practice bare living merely as a moral exercise: he wanted to obey Emerson's dictum to save on the low levels and spend on the high ones. It is this that distinguishes him from the tedious people whose whole existence is absorbed in the practice of living on beans, or breathing deeply, or wearing clothes of a vegetable origin: simplification did not lead in Thoreau to the cult of simplicity: it led to a higher civilization.

What drove Thoreau to the solitude of the woods was no cynical contempt for the things beyond his reach. "Before we can adorn our houses with beautiful objects, the walls must be stripped, and our lives must be stripped, and beautiful housekeeping and beautiful living be laid for a foundation: now, a taste for the beautiful is most cultivated out of doors, where there is no house, and no housekeeper." The primeval woods were a favorable beginning for the search; but Thoreau did not think they could be the end of it. The land itself, however, did stir his imagination; he wrote:

> *All things invite this earth's inhabitants*
> *To rear their lives to an unheard of height,*
> *And meet the expectation of the land.*

"The expectation of the land!" One comes upon that phrase, or its equivalent, in almost every valid piece of early American thought. One thinks of moorland pastures by the sea, dark with bayberries and sweet fern, breaking out among the lichened rocks; and the tidal rivers bringing their weedy tang to the low meadows, wide and open in the sun; the purple pine groves, where the needles, bedded deep, hum to the wind, or the knotted New England hills, where the mountain laurel in June seems like upland snow, left over, or where the marble breaks through into clusters of perpetual laurel and everlasting;

one sees mountain lakes, giant aquamarines, sapphires, topazes, and upland pastures where the blue, purple, lavender and green of the huckleberry bushes give way in autumn to the fringe of sumach by the roadside, volcanoes of reds and crimsons; the yellow of September cornfields, with intenser pumpkins lying between the shocks, or the naked breasts and flanks of the autumn landscape, quivering in uneasy sleep before the white blanket puts it to rest. To smell this, taste this, and feel and climb and walk over this landscape, once untouched, like an unopened letter or a lover unkissed—who would not rise to meet the expectation of the land? Partly, it was the challenge of babyhood: how will it grow up and what will become of it? Partly, it was the charm of innocence; or again, it was the sense of the mighty variety that the whole continent gives, as if between the two oceans every possible human habitat might be built, and every conceivable variety of experience fathomed.

What the aboriginal Indian had absorbed from the young earth, Thoreau absorbed; what the new settlers had given her, the combing of the plow, the cincture of the stone fence or the row of planted elms, these things he absorbed too; for Thoreau, having tasted the settled life of Concord, knew that the wilderness was not a permanent home for man: one might go there for fortification, for a quickening of the senses, for a tightening of all the muscles; but that, like any retreat, is a special exercise and wants a special occasion: one returned to Nature in order to become, in a deeper sense, more cultivated and civilized, not in order to return to crudities that men had already discarded. Looking ahead, Thoreau saw what was needed to preserve the valuable heritage of the American wilderness. He wrote:

"The kings of England formerly had their forests to hold the king's game, for sport or food, sometimes destroying villages to create and extend them; and I think that they were impelled by a true instinct. Why should not we, who have renounced the king's authority, have our national preserves, where no villages need be destroyed, in which the bear and panther, and some even of the hunter race, may still exist, and not be 'civilized off the face of the earth,'—our own forests, not to hold the king's game merely, but to hold and preserve the king himself also, the

lord of creation,—and not in idle sport of food, but for inspira-
tion and our own true recreation? or shall we, like the villains,
grub them all up, poaching on our own national domain?"

These pregnant suggestions of Thoreau, which were to be
embodied only after two generations in our National and State
Parks, and in projects like Mr. Benton Mackaye's great conception of the Appalachian trail, make the comments of those who
see in him only an arch-individualist, half-Diogenes, half-
Rousseau, seem a little beside the point. The individualism of
an Emerson or a Thoreau was the necessary complement of the
thoroughly socialized existence of the New England town; it was
what prevented these towns from becoming collections of yes-
men, with never an opinion or an emotion that differed from
their neighbors. He wrote for his fellow-townsmen; and his notion of the good life was one that should carry to a higher pitch
the existing polity and culture of Concord itself. "As the nobleman of cultivated taste surrounds himself with whatever con-
duces to his culture—genius—learning—wit—books—paintings
—statuary—music—philosophical instruments, and the like; so
let the village do—not stop short at a pedagogue, a parson, a sex-
ton, a parish library, and three selectmen, because our pilgrim
forefathers got through a cold winter once on a bleak rock with
these. To act collectively is according to the spirit of our institutions; and I am confident that, as our circumstances are more
flourishing, our means are greater than the nobleman's." Do
not those sentences alter a little our stereotype of homespun
New England, of Individualistic America?

Just as Thoreau sought Nature, in order to arrive at a higher
state of culture, so he practiced individualism, in order to create a better order of society. Taking America as it was, Thoreau conceived a form, a habitat, which would retain what was
unique in the American contact with the virgin forest, the cultivated soil, and the renewed institutions of the New England
town. He understood the precise thing that the pioneer lacked.
The pioneer had exhausted himself in a senseless external activity, which answered no inner demands except those for oblivion.
In his experiment at Walden Pond, Thoreau "learned this, at
least . . . that if one advances confidently in the direction of

his dreams, and endeavors to live the life which he has imagined, he will meet with success unexpected in the common hours. . . . In proportion as he simplifies his life, the laws of the universe will appear less complex, and solitude will not be solitude, nor poverty poverty, nor weakness weakness. If you have built castles in the air, your work need not be lost; that is where they should be. Now put the foundations under them."

In short, Thoreau lived in his desires; in rational and beautiful things that he imagined worth doing, and did. The pioneer lived only in extraneous necessities; and he vanished with their satisfaction: filling all the conditions of his environment, he never fulfilled himself. With the same common ground between them in their initial feeling towards Nature, Thoreau and the pioneer stood at opposite corners of the field. What Thoreau left behind is still precious; men may still go out and make over America in the image of Thoreau. What the pioneer left behind, alas! was only the burden of a vacant life.

HIGH NOON

v

"HE that by me spreads a wider breast than my own proves the width of my own." So Walt Whitman chanted in the Song of Myself; and in the greatness of Whitman the genius of Emerson was justified. Walt Whitman was a cosmos: he was inclusive where Emerson and Thoreau were restrictive: he was sensual and jolly where they were refined and taut: he identified himself with the mere bulk and vastness of the American continent, and, with a tremendous appetite for the actual, entered into the experience of the pioneer, the roadhand, the mechanic, the woodman, the soldier, the farmer. In some remote Dutch ancestor of Whitman's one figures the men and women of Franz Hals's portraiture, people large, lusty, loving, men who like their sweetheart and their steak, women who give themselves to love as the flower bows to the weight of the bee. With Emerson, to repeat the obvious, one surveys the world from a glacial summit: the air is rarefied, and at the distance even the treacherous places in the landscape seem orderly and innocent. With Whitman one sees the heights from the bosom of the valley: the "unseen is proved by the seen, till that becomes unseen, and receives proofs of its own."

Whitman absorbed so much of the America about him, that he is more than a single writer: he is almost a literature. Pushing his way like some larval creature through one husk after another, through the hard shell of Puritanism, in which he wrote Temperance Tracts, through the shell of republicanism in which he glorified all the new political institutions, through the flimsy casement of romantic poetry, iridescent with cheap colors and empty rhymes, Whitman finally achieved his own metamorphosis, and emerged, with dripping wings, into the untempered mid-day of the American scene. The stages of this metamorphosis have created contradictions in Whitman's work; and if we are to appreciate his full achievement, we must be ready to throw aside the vestiges of his larval state.

First, there was in Whitman a certain measure of the political religiosity of Joel Barlow and Philip Freneau. Political nationalism, in certain aspects of Whitman's thought, assumed a mystical beauty and centrality: he wrote about the United States as if they were the tissue of men's eternal desires—as if the robbery of Mexican territory, for example, could be justified to the Mexicans as well as the Americans by the inevitable drag of our Manifest Destiny. Here Whitman was confusing spiritual with temporal dominion. He had conceived new spiritual patterns, appropriate to the modern, which were to be fulfilled in the America of his dreams; and it was hard to resist identifying this hope of a wider America with the expansionist activities of political bandits. In this mood, to speak frankly, Whitman ranted.

Nevertheless, when one sums up Whitman's observations upon the Union and upon the political state of the country, no one surely ever ranted with so many reservations; and it is unfair to take the bombastic lines out of the context that perpetually qualifies them. The political reality that was so precious to Whitman was only a means of permitting the growth of "superb persons," and a life, "copious, vehement, spiritual, bold." Moreover, between the Walt Whitman who wrote the original Leaves of Grass, and the defeated and paralyzed man who lingered on through the Gilded Age, there is a difference; and by 1879 Whitman had come to realize that his democracy was one that had been based on free land and equal opportunity to use it, and that failure was beginning to threaten the political structure. "If the United States," he wrote, "like the countries of the Old World, are also to grow vast crops of poor, desperate, dissatisfied, nomadic, miserably waged populations, such as we see looming upon us of late years—steadily, even if slowly, eating into them like a cancer of lungs or stomach—then our republican experiment, notwithstanding all its surface-successes, is at heart an unhealthy failure. . . ." That was not all. "By the unprecedented open-up of humanity enmasse in the United States in the last hundred years, under our institutions, not only the good qualities of the race, but just as much the bad ones, are prominently brought forward. Man is about the same, in the main, whether with despotism or whether with freedom."

That saving and irrefragable common sense was what ballasted all of Whitman's hopes and expectations. He lived to see the America he dreamed of undermined and rotten: he saw the Kings of Iron and Oil and Cotton supplant not merely the older ones who ruled by divine right but the new one elected quadrennially by the people: he saw the diverse but well-mixed America of his youth give way to the America of the melting pot, which neither welded the old nationalities nor had the spiritual power to create a new one: he saw the sickly barbers and perfumers of the New York literary schools of the forties turn into the gentlemanly tailors who cut their stories and their thoughts to fit the fat paunches of the middle classes in the seventies: he saw all this, and denied nothing. No critic ferreted out the weaknesses and pettinesses of America with a surer nose than Whitman tracked them down in his Democratic Vistas: what could be said against his dream, Whitman said, with the staunch candor of a friend. But his thought and his vision were unshaken; the promise of America had not disappeared. If it was absent from the immediate scene, it had nevertheless taken form in his poems; and his poems were still waiting to shape a new America.

In Leaves of Grass Whitman had fulfilled Emerson in more ways than either of them suspected. There are passages of Emerson's prose which have, potentially, the prosody of Whitman; but whereas Emerson's poems, at their best, remain fragmentary and broken, because the meaning was somehow always warping the metes and measures Emerson respected and clung to, in Whitman, at his best, these new thoughts find their own beat, and become poetry of the first rank. Whitman had discovered Emerson's inner form in creating his own. He himself had stammered and stuttered so long as he kept to the old metres: his early work was weak and sentimental because he had nothing to say within the bounds of those previous culture-molds which Whitman tagged as "feudal." New streams of thought and experience were confluent in Whitman: the *Weltanschauung* of Hegel, precursor of the evolutionists, who saw the world as a continual becoming, and both the bad and the good as part of the total meaning of the universe; the electric doctrine of Emerson, which bade every man find his own center and every institution to answer up for its results in one's own life; the unstratified society of America, where the bus driver was as good as the next man, and the private soldier as great as the statesman whose policies reduced him to a pawn; the cleansing operations of science, which confronted every variety in thought, and made no more distinction between the clean and the unclean, the minute and the immense, than some indifferent deity, for whom the fall of a gnat and the fall of an Empire are of precisely the same importance. Out of the discussions of the Fourierists, and the societies of Free Lovers, and women who pressed for the political and social emancipation of their sex, as well as out of his own capacious adventures, Whitman got the courage to deal with the varieties of sexual experience, too: in the Children of Adam and Calamus he brushed past the nice restraints of Emerson—who "held his nose" at its passages – and Thoreau, who, like Natty Bumppo and Paul Bunyan, averted himself from any passion more intense than friendship.

Whitman took in the quaker, the puritan, the cosmopolitan, the pioneer, the republican; and what came out in his poems was none of these things: it was a new essence; none of the ordinary labels described it. It had the smell of reality which was science; it had the largeness of comprehension which was philosophy; and it had the doubts, searchings, quests, achievements, and consummations which are the stuff of life itself. Whitman found no need to add an extra dimension to his experience: to transcribe for him was in the highest sense to *translate*. Whatever tended to create full-bodied and full-minded men and women tended toward enlarging the significance of every single activity, no matter how base or minute. The veil of appearance was as mysterious and beautiful as anything behind the veil. Perhaps it was all Maya, all illusion; or perhaps life was like a set of Chinese boxes: one removed the outer box of appearance, and discovered another box—appearance. What of it? A single blade of grass was enough to confound all the atheists; and whatever else the universe might hold, he reckoned that there was no sweeter meat than that which clung to his own bones. Such faith does not need external props and certitudes: it mocks at the testimony of bibles, for it is itself the source of such testimony.

People have hesitated to call Whitman's poems poetry; it is useless to deny that they belong to sacred literature. If the Leaves of Grass are not poetry, it is only because not every generation endows us with such a poet.

VI

Literature may be evocative or formative: one plays upon sentiments, emotions, ideas that already exist: the other changes the very attitude of the audience, and calls new ones forth. The common American of the Golden Day responded to Longfellow and Whittier; for these men caught his ordinary mood, measured off and rhymed; and even when Whittier and Lowell wrote on abolition themes, they were only touching strings which a Garrison or a Wendell Phillips had already set in motion. It is amusing to note the way in which ante-bellum America responded to Whitman. Emerson and Thoreau were quick to see his genius, even to proclaim it. Lesser people, however, like Moncure Conway, were a little disappointed in him: they expected to find in Whitman the common workman, grown vocal, some one who could be taken into society and patronized; some one who would bolster up their notion of a poet who had risen from the lowly ranks.

Whitman was not a democrat, in the sense of being a popular mediocrity; he was a man of genius; who, mid all his school teaching, editing, carpentering, type-setting and what-not remained consecrated to the profession of letters: Jesus Son of Sirach was no more certain of his vocation. Whitman was Pygmalion to his own Galatea: he had formed himself, so that he might give a new model to America. The imperturbable landscape, the satisfaction and aplomb of animals, the ecstasy of hearty lovers, the meditations of one who sits withdrawn in the crowd, or on a mountain top—Whitman extracted from these things a new shape, which was himself. Every poem of Whitman's is the man; every part of the man threw forth tendrils which clung to the objects of poems. One could not become a sympathetic reader of Whitman without re-forming oneself into an approximation of this new shape. Only commonplace works of art reflect the everyday personality of the reader: the supreme works always show or hint of the new shape the reader may become: they are prophetic, formative. One might remove Longfellow without changing a single possibility of American life; had Whitman died in the cradle, however, the possibilities of American life would have been definitely impoverished. He created a new pattern of experience and character. The work he conceived still remains to be done: the America he evoked does not as yet exist.

Whitman was a poet in the braid Scots sense of makkar: a maker or creator. He was conscious of the fact that the accumulated culture of Europe had lost a good part of its original meaning, through lack of direct contact with the new forces of discovery, science, democracy: the work of the old makkars was crumbling away; at best, it was repeated by rote, as in the churches, without any sense of the living reality, or the finer passages were rolled on the tongue, for sensation's sake, by an aristocratic minority. "Note to-day," Whitman observed in Democratic Vistas, "a curious spectacle and conflict. . . . Science, testing absolutely all thoughts, all works, has already burst well upon the world

—a sun, mounting, most illuminating, most glorious, surely never again to set. But against it, deeply entrenched, holding possession, yet remains (not only through the churches and schools but by imaginative literature and unregenerate poetry) the fossil theology of the mythic-materialistic superstitious, untaught and credulous, fable-loving primitive ages of humanity."

Whitman saw that the office of sacred literature was no longer being performed; or at all events, that those who were pursuing it were not fully conscious of either the need or the opportunity. Vulgar literature was, indeed, growing hugely. "To-day, in books, in the rivalry of writers, especially novelists, success (so-called) is for him or her who strikes the mean flat average, the sensational appetite for stimulus, incident, persiflage, etc., and depicts to the common caliber, sensual, exterior life." What remained of sacred literature was insufficient to offset this. It was to establish a central point in literature, in terms of science and the modern, that Whitman created: American poetry was to do in our day what the Vedas, the Nackas, the Talmud, the Old Testament, the Gospel, Plato's works had done for their time: it was to crystallize our most precious experience and in turn to modify, by that act of crystallization, the daily routine.

What, in fact, were the active formative literatures when Whitman wrote? In the Western World the principal one was, without doubt, that great miscellany called the Old Testament, supplemented by the gospels; and among the cultivated classes, Homer, Horace, Plutarch, Dante, Shakespeare, Corneille, played a lively but minor part. The Romantic movement, which went back to the ballads and the folk-literature of the various regions of Europe was a recognition of the fact that something was lacking in both the Hebrew and the classic traditions, and in the literature which was directly founded upon them. What was lacking was the direct historic connection with a people, a place, and a special way of life. It is true that all literature has certain common characters, and no great works of the spirit are foreign and remote; but, as Whitman pointed out, "something is rooted in the invisible roots, the profoundest meanings, of a place, race, or nationality," and the Romantic movement had cut loose from classic and Hebraic influences in order to absorb this more intimate order of meaning and find a nearer and fresher source of spiritual activity. Blake, Keats, Shelley, had partly achieved this; Wordsworth alone, however, had created new forms without relying on a mythic-materialistic past.

With what was universal in all these efforts, Whitman could sympathize: Homer and Shakespeare and the Bible had been his daily food. He sought to do for common men and women, for the contemporary and the ordinary-heroic, what Shakespeare had achieved in his great images of the aristocratic life. In America, in modern life, on the farm and in the laboratory, in the progress of souls along the grand roads of the Universe, in company with the Great Companions, the swift and majestic men, the capacious and broad-bosomed women—here was the stuff for new Vedas, Cycles, and Testaments. Whitman overvalued, if anything, the contrivances of political democracy; but that was only a first step; he overcountenanced, if anything, the absorption of America in materialistic effort; that, however, was only the second step. Neither political democracy nor industrial progress was for him anything but a prelude to the third stage, rising out of the two previous ones, and creating a "native expression spirit" and an abundance of rich personalities.

In his effort to keep ballasted and always find a landing place in contemporary existence, Whitman was perhaps too receptive and undiscriminating in his acknowledgement of current values and aims; in his old age, he accepted with child-like delight the evidences of material prosperity he found on his Western trip. His Hegelianism was dangerous stuff: it led him to identify the Real and the Ideal, instead of seeing, as William James put it, that they were dynamically continuous. But at the core, Whitman was never deceived: he knew that the meaning of all current activity lay only in the forms or symbols it created and the rational purposes it embodied; and so far from believing that the work of the poet or artist would be supplanted by science, he believed that "the highest and subtlest and broadest truths of modern science wait for their true assignment and last vivid flashes of light—as Democracy waits for its—through first-class metaphysicians and speculative philosophs—laying the basements and foundations for these new, more expanded, more harmonious, more melodious, freer American poems." To indicate these new meanings, to open up these new relationships, Whitman wrote his poems. I can think of no one in whom the unconscious and the conscious process worked more in harmony: the life and the doctrine were one. So far as Whitman went, he achieved his end.

So far as he went! Most people are unaware that the Leaves of Grass, Calamus, the Children of Adam, are only a part of the vast canvas he projected; they do not realize that he was diverted from his original intention and never lived to complete it. The Leaves of Grass were to deal chiefly with the palpable and the material; there was to be a complementary volume which would center mainly on the spiritual and the in-actual—upon death and immortality and final meanings—for he was the poet of the body and he was the poet of the soul. Alas! the Civil War came. He threw himself into it as a hospital visitor, giving his personality and his radiant health to the sick and the wounded, as these men had given themselves in the camp and on the battlefield. Within a few years this ordeal exacted its revenge: he became paralyzed, and as he never fully recovered his physical powers, his mental powers diminished, too: if they are still at their summit in Drum-Taps, they recurred only fitfully in the later poems: and though he could outline his aspiration with a firm hand in Democratic Vistas, published in 1871, he could no longer model it and round it out. What he meant to create is implied in all his poems; the whole of it was never, perhaps, expressed.

Whitman himself had felt that the War for the American Union was the Odyssey of his generation; but except for himself and Herman Melville, no one lived to write about it in those terms; the stories of Ambrose Bierce, Stephen Crane, and Upton Sinclair did not treat it in this vein. Whitman did not see that the great conflict might have a Punic ending. As it turned out, the war was a struggle between two forms of servitude, the slave and the machine. The machine won, and the human spirit was almost as much paralyzed by the victory as it would have been by the defeat. An industrial transformation took place over night: machines were applied to agriculture;

they produced new guns and armaments; the factory regime, growing tumultuously in the Eastern cities, steadily undermined the balanced regimen of agriculture and industry which characterized the East before the war.

The machines won; and the war kept on. Its casualties were not always buried at Antietam or Gettysburg; they moldered, too, in libraries, studies, offices. The justifiable ante-bellum optimism of Emerson turned into a waxen smile. Whitman lost his full powers in what should have been his prime. Among the young men, many a corpse was left, to go through the routine of living. But before the Golden Day was over, the American mind had lived through a somber and beautiful hour, the hour of Hawthorne and Melville. With them, the sun turned to a candle, and cast black shadows upon the wall, not the empty grotesque shadows of Poe, but the shapes of a magnified if distorted humanity.

TWILIGHT

VII

HAWTHORNE was the afterglow of the Seventeenth Century. With him came the twilight of Puritanism as a spiritual force. Presently, it became altogether a handy servant of industry, and as a system of ideas, ceased to be interesting or to attract interesting minds. Men like Josiah Royce, born some fifty years after Hawthorne, became, in the jargon of philosophy, absolute idealists; those who did not take this path flourished in negations. Puritanism left its mark on America after the Civil War chiefly through its code of inhibitions and avoidances; in this sense, it is still with us. In Hawthorne, however, the conviction which produced a Paradise Lost or a Pilgrim's Progress still glowed with a white intensity; but its heat was gone. Hawthorne was silver; the silver of moonlight; the silver of fine goblets; the tarnished silver of ancient and abandoned houses, locked in moldy drawers.

Hawthorne was no longer frightened by the bogies of the Puritan hell; but his interest in human weakness and its consequences remained: he was an esthetician of sin. Into the shadows of Seventeenth Century New England, with a consciousness that remained outwardly Puritan, he projected the figures of his own day. One does not perhaps recognize in the Scarlet Letter and in the The House of the Seven Gables the torments of the modern consciousness; but they are there. Pull off the costumes and look closely at these Hesters and Hepzibahs: they are sisters of the Annas and Nastasyas that the great Russians are portraying. Did you think that the Scarlet Letter was placed upon the waxen breast of a dummy? Do not be deceived. The flesh is tender, and the heart beats. The characters in Hawthorne's principal tragedy were both symbolic and real: Chillingworth was a vengeful, impotent old man: he was also a deterministic Puritanism, caught within its materialist circle, and unable to take possession of life, to which it had been too lately and grudgingly wedded. The young minister was a sweet, neurotic soul, impotent through conflict, where Chillingworth was impotent through denial: he was the prototype of the Ruskins and Amiels who haunted the century: he was likewise the figure of a weak and spindly idealism which faints at the first warm breath of reality, and dare not acknowledge the child it has begotten. Hester need not forfeit her own existence to become the creative spirit itself, breaking away from the Puritanic bond, unsatisfied by the temporary union with Transcendentalism—it did not take Hawthorne long to discover the insufficiency of Brook Farm—and living out, with a single child, a destiny without husband or lover.

I have perhaps read too freely into the fable: Hawthorne himself had no such conscious purpose as that I have been trying to explicate: but the novel will bear pondering: it is no mere study of the external rigors of an abandoned creed. If I err, I am absurd in the same way that Hawthorne himself was, when he made a note of a gas main that lay beneath a whole city, and wondered whether it might not be made the symbol of some widespread but secret evil. At heart, the American novelists were all transcendental. The scene was a symbol: they scarcely had the patience to describe it: they were interested in it only because it pointed to something more important. Even Poe, who sneered at Concord, was equally an imaginative Transcendentalist: Mardi and the Fall of the House of Usher, and the Scarlet Letter were all of one brood. These writers were lost in the inactual: sin, death, eternity—these held their minds, not "chops and tomato sauce"!

There is a tragic moment in all experience, which good health cannot overcome, which good institutions cannot avert. Hawthorne was conscious of this inescapable thread of evil, and delighted in the complicated arabesque it presents to the mind when traced over the whole tapestry of existence. Sometimes the evil appeared to him as heredity, as it does with the Jews; sometimes it is fate, more dumb and irremediable—a life which has not faced this lurking and inscrutable malevolence has only made a childish reckoning of its possibilities. Hawthorne followed its last intricacy with the patience of a physiologist lingering over a microscopic slide of morbid tissue. What could the professional optimists make of this doctrine? Was it not just the clammy perspiration left on the walls of old New England buildings? Would it not be removed by central heating, a fresh coat of paint, or some other external improvement? Who could believe that life presented inherent evils which no mechanical improvements would diminish: who dared to believe this as long as the population of New Eden doubled every five years, and real-estate values kept going up?

The possibilities of tragic experience in America were passing away, even when Hawthorne was writing. There was no tragedy in the program of the pioneer and the industrialist: there was just success or disappointment, whereas tragedy shows the canker that rots success, and the depth of a sorrow that belittles disappointment; doing so, it summons up that greatness of spirit in which Hester, for example, faces life, once her most painful part has been acted out. There is no surer test of the quality of life in what I have called the Golden Day, than the two tragedies, The Scarlet Letter and Moby Dick, which issued out of it. The sunlight had in Emerson and Whitman penetrated to every spot, and in its presence, the dark corners became more intense. If one explored the white summits of the glacier with Emerson, one might also fall into the abyss with

Melville. One climbed high; and when one fell, the fall was deep.

NIGHT

VIII

The waters that unite the continents of the world once meant more to the thin strip of communities that lined that Atlantic coast than the prairies where the buffalo wandered. Sloops and catboats plied the inlets and the rivers, bungs and schooners went up and down the coast; and at last, after a hundred years of boat-building, the clipper-ship, designed in the shipyards of New York and Boston and Newburyport and Portland, began to scud dangerously over the seas, carrying ice cut during the winter on Walden Pond or Fresh Pond to cool the merchant of Calcutta, picking up cargoes of teas and silks, or venturing out from Long Island or New Bedford, to stay years on the water in pursuit of the whale.

A lad leaves his schoolmates, and at twenty navigates his father's ship; a girl sails with her husband, nurses him during a difficult illness, and brings the ship safely to port, making all the reckonings herself; in the long watches, as the ship sails on even keel, the mind is open to new thoughts and fresh insights: Morse invents his telegraph aboard ship, and Colt makes a wooden model of the deadly revolver: those who are more reflective than ingenious mix their thoughts with adventure and derring-do: a ship opens the mind of a young lawyer named Dana, and it never opens so satisfactorily again: life on board ship is the beginning of Henry George's intellectual adventure.

Every year these quiet inlets launched their ships; the clipper was the supreme esthetic achievement of the day and land, better by far than current architecture or painting; and, unlike the covered wagon, these vessels returned. On board and in port, the beauty and brutality of the life mingled, the strength and the arrogance and the hardness and whipcord skill, the bullying, the petty meanness, the greed, the concupiscence, the fierce press of work in a storm contrasted with the occasions of sweet profound apathy, the immensity of quiet nights under the stars, and the hot pressure of strange courtesans, flagrant with perfumes, in the little houses one might stumble upon in the bazaars of Colombo or Canton. Put all this over against the measured, fussy life of New York or Baltimore, respectable, sensible, at bottom banal and sordid. Such heights and such depths! He who had touched them knew too well that no mean could be golden!

Herman Melville, born in New York in the same year as Whitman, mixed of the same Dutch-English stock, dying, too, within a year of Whitman, Herman Melville turned to the sea, and, in the great age of our seamanship, tasted for himself the qualities of both Odysseus and Homer. From his personal adventures, after he had jumped ship in the South Seas, he wrote that fine idyll of the tropics called Typee. Face to face with the savages of the Marquesas, he discovered that in mere joyousness of life, civilization had nothing to endow a man with that these ferocious and innocent cannibals did not possess: on the contrary, considered merely as animal existence, there was a more beautiful and exuberant animality in the savage state than in the hard pragmatic routine of our urban money-warrens. While he stuck to the sea, the whaler, the merchantman, and the man-of-war each made their contribution to Melville. Finally, at the age of thirty, he gathered himself for a great effort: the result was the epic poem called Moby Dick.

The quality of Moby Dick and the fate of Moby Dick throw an interesting light upon the cast of mind that characterized the age. After the usual brief success Melville's books almost all enjoyed, it was tossed aside, to eke out an existence as a boy's book of adventure. Swift's satire had met the same fate, and for the same reason: adults who wish to prolong their infantile state turn books like this over to children upon whom the deeper fable can make no impression, whilst they themselves take comfort in books that are written out of a more puerile consciousness. That Moby Dick was not recognized, except here and there by an isolated critic, as a great book, is due to the fact, I think, that Moby Dick is poetry. The jolly and comfortable bourgeois tradition of the Victorian age, a state of mind composed of felt slippers and warm bellywash, could not produce such a work: the genius of its great writers, its Dickenses and Thackerays, was of quite another cut. To find a parallel for Moby Dick one must go back to Dekker, Heywood, Webster, Marlowe, and Thomas Browne; men who translated the drab events of the outer life into a wild and passionate dialect of their own. These are the kin of Melville. His prose, too, had the richness of the early Seventeenth Century, capable of great rhythms, always ready to float easily off the sandbars of commonplace description and out onto the rolling waters of the grand style. In Whitman and Melville letters again became as racy as the jabber of a waterside saloon; in all of Poe's poetry there is scarcely a line as good as pages of the best of Melville's prose.

Moby Dick was not merely poetry; it was a product of that deep meditation on the world and life and time which makes philosophy; and among the treasures of the book is a single paragraph which might claim a place beside whole treatises on the central problems of destiny, fate, free-will. I cannot forbear putting it down. It takes rise from an afternoon on which Melville was calmly performing one of the routine functions of the ship, the making of a mat.

"As I kept on passing and repassing the filling or woof of marline between the long yarns of the warp, using my hand for the shuttle . . . it seemed as if this were the Loom of Time, and I myself were a shuttle mechanically weaving away at the Fates. There lay the fixed threads of the warp subject to but one single, ever-returning, unceasing vibration, and that vibration merely enough to admit of the crosswise interbinding of other threads with its own. The warp seemed necessity, and here, thought I, with my own hand I ply my own shuttle and weave my own destiny into these unalterable threads. Meantime, Queequeg's impulsive, indifferent sword, sometimes hitting the woof slantingly, or crookedly, or strongly, or weakly, as the case might be; and by this difference in the concluding blow producing a corresponding contrast in the final aspect of the completed fabric; this savage's sword, thought I, which thus finally shapes and fashions both warp and woof; this easy, indifferent sword must be chance—aye, chance, free will, and necessity—nowise incompatible—all interweavingly working together. The straight warp of necessity, not to be swerved from its ultimate course—its ever alternating vibration, indeed, only tending to that; free will still free to ply the shuttle between given threads; and chance, though restricted in its play within the right lines of necessity, and sideways in its motions directed by free will, though thus prescribed to by both, chance by turn rules either, and has the last featuring blow at events."

If this generation did not produce any skilled professional philosophers, I am not sure that it altogether lacked the living stuff of philosophy.

Melville, who was a friend and neighbor of Hawthorne in the Berkshires, once wrote into an enthusiastic description of Hawthorne's work a true picture of his own. "There is a certain tragic phase of humanity which, in our opinion, was never more powerfully embodied than by Hawthorne. We mean the tragedies of human thought in its own unbiased, native, and profounder working. We think that in no recorded mind has the intense feeling of the visible truth ever entered more deeply than into this man's. By visible truth we mean the apprehension of the absolute condition of present things as they strike the eye of the man who fears them not, though they do their worst to him,—the man who, like Russia or the British Empire, declares himself a sovereign nature (in himself) amid the powers of heaven, hell, and earth. He may perish; but so long as he exists he insists upon treating with all Powers upon an equal basis."

The absolute condition of present things was what Melville sought to track down in the fable and the myth of the White Whale. One may read Moby Dick as a story of the sea, and be irritated by the lengthy description of whales and whaling; one may read it as a treatise on the whaling industry, and be irritated by the irrelevant heroic figure of Ahab, or the innocent sinister beauty of Queequeg; and since it is also this, one may read it as an epic of the human spirit, and discover an equivalent of its symbolism in one's own consciousness. For me, the Whale is Nature, the Nature man warily hunts and subdues, the Nature he captures, tethers to his ship, cuts apart, scientifically analyzes, melts down, uses for light and nourishment, sells in the market, the Nature that serves man's purposes so long as he uses his wits and can ride on top. But with all this easy adventuring, there is another and deadlier Nature—the White Whale—a Nature that threatens man and calls forth all his heroic powers, and in the end defeats him with a final lash of the tail. That part of Nature cannot be harpooned, cannot be captured, still less drawn and quartered and sold. In sheer savagery—or was it perhaps in play?—the White Whale had once amputated Ahab's leg: with relentless vigilance Ahab follows the White Whale to its lair, impatient of baser catches on the way, as the great philosophers and poets have been impatient of the little harpoonings and dickerings of science and the practical life. The White Whale is not the kindly, milk-fed Absolute, in which all conflicts are reconciled and all contradictions united into a higher kind of knowledge; no, the White Whale is the sheer brute energy of the universe, which challenges and checks the spirit of man. It is only the lonely heroic spirit, who declares himself a sovereign nature, that dares follow the White Whale; and once he comes to close quarters with the creature, there is no issue but death. The White Whale is the external force of Nature and Destiny. In the end it conquers: it must conquer: until the spirit of man is itself Leviathan, and can meet its antagonist on even terms.

In Moby Dick Melville carried the private voyage of the soul to its inevitable conclusion. Men are sustained, in faith and work, not by what they find in the universe, but by what man has built there. Man gave the word: he gave the symbol: he gave the form: he believed in his ejaculations and created language; he believed in his forms and wrought cities; he believed in his symbols, and created myth, poetry, science, philosophy. Deny this initial act of faith, tear aside the veil man has thrown between his own experience and the blank reality of the universe and everything else becomes meaningless: depend upon one's private self alone and though the renunciation be heroic, the result is inevitable: the White Whale will swallow one at a gulp. To appreciate the reality of the White Whale is to see more deeply into the expedience of all our intermediate institutions, all the spiritual shelters man puts between himself and the uncertain cosmic weather. Meaning, significance, attends only that little part of the universe man has built up and settled; the South Sea Islander, in his lazy and primitive culture, had achieved this meaning and lived happily; Melville, having divested himself of the meanings man had wrought and faced the universe as a sovereign power, was confronted by a blank: he peered behind the curtain, and heard the dim rattle of his breath echoing through the abyss: nothing was there! So far can the spirit go by itself; no farther. If it returns at all, it is back to the common life.

On the imaginative level of Moby Dick Melville never again walked: he had exhausted himself. In his short-stories, he pictured himself more than once as an old man; and at thirty he was already that. There are tortured fragments of Melville in Mardi and Pierre; but the depth and bottom of the man had been sounded in Moby Dick. From that time on he lived in a sort of mechanical dream. His marriage, his wandering through the Near East, his interest in the Civil War—none of these could heal his spirit. He succumbed to rheumatism and the burden of supporting his family; the greater part of his manhood he clung tenaciously, like a ghost rattling his chains, to the post in the Customs House at Gansevoort Street. Fame, ambitions, friends, travel, love, nothing was left him in all this; he had exhausted their possibilities before he was thirty-five.

For thirty years Melville was like the dead man of Poe's, whose processes of decomposition were halted. He died twice: nothing in the drab and dapper America after the Civil War could recall him to the advantages of an earthly existence. The forms and activities of the new day—what were they? Could he look upon Howells as his son; could he treat Mark Twain as an equal? "Life," Hawthorne had written, "is made up of marble and mud." Melville, who had so superbly shaped the marble, was unable to do anything with the mud, or rather, he let the mud overwhelm him, and sank into it deeper and deeper. The American had faced the tragedy of the White Whale. He was now to retire to nearer and shallower waters. Emerson, Thoreau, Whitman, Melville, yes, and Hawthorne had answered the challenge of American experience. Presently, their heroic words will be forgotten, and their successors, living corpses, too, will look back to the days of their youth, as to a dream, real only while it lasted.

Chapter Four   The Pragmatic Acquiescence

I

THE Civil War arose in a mess of muddy issues. The abolitionists' attack upon slavery, full of moral righteousness and oblivious to the new varieties of slavery that were being practiced under industrialism, stiffened the South into a spasm even more self-righteous, even more blind. Twenty years of fierce debate found the Southerner frequently denying that the Negro was a human being: it also found the abolitionist denying that the slaveholder was a human being. In that temper, all the rational humane people who were searching for effective measures to reduce the area of slavery and pension off the institution found their hands tied and their throats throttled. The South fought to preserve slavery by extending its territory: the answer to this was natural: and then, to muddle matters worse, the issue was mixed up with Centralism versus State's Rights. There were honest abolitionists who desired that the Union should break up into a Slave State and a Free State which would serve as a biblical city of refuge; there were slavery men who were reluctant to see the Union destroyed.

The smoke of warfare blinded the issue further. When it cleared away, the slave question had disappeared but the "Negro question" remained; and in the inevitable dictatorship of war, the central government, particularly the Executive, emerged, mystically raising aloft the Union as a mask for all its depredations. What the office-holders in the central government called "the menace of sectionalism," and what we may call equally "the promise of regionalism" was exterminated for fully two generations. Local life declined. The financial centers grew: through the mechanism of finance, New York and Chicago began to dominate the rest of the country. Presently the novel of "local color" appeared—proof enough that the color had washed out.

The Civil War cut a white gash through the history of the country; it dramatized in a stroke the changes that had begun to take place during the preceding twenty or thirty years. On one side lay the Golden Day, the period of an Elizabethan daring on the sea, of a well-balanced adjustment of farm and factory in the East, of a thriving regional culture, operating through the lecture-lyceum and the provincial college; an age in which the American mind had flourished and had begun to find itself. When the curtain rose on the post-bellum scene, this old America was for all practical purposes demolished: industrialism had entered overnight, had transformed the practices of agriculture, had encouraged a mad exploitation of mineral oil, natural gas, and coal, and had made the unscrupulous master of finance, fat with war-profits, the central figure of the situation. All the crude practices of British paleotechnic industry appeared on the new scene without relief or mitigation.

On both sides of the line many a fine lad had died in battle, and those who survived, in more subtle ways died, too. Some of them had evaded the opportunity for physical death: Mark Twain, after a brief anomalous period in the army, ran away to Nevada, William Dean Howells accepted a consular post in Venice, Stanley Hall, honest enough to record the point in his autobiography, accepted the services of a paid substitute. Happy the dead! The period after the war was the Gilded Age, with a vengeance. Sidney Lanier, who had served the South, and emerged a skeleton, faced the bitter truth of this great outburst of material enterprise:

> "Trade is trade but sings a lie:
> 'Tis only war grown miserly."

Unchecked, unmodified, industrialism controlled the mind as well as the material apparatus of the country: men who had a cut for scholarship, like Charles Francis Adams, became railroad magnates, and the son of the Great Emancipator became the head of the Pullman Corporation. H. G. Eastman founded the business school in 1855, and by the end of the war that which was established in Poughkeepsie had more than a thousand pupils. The Massachusetts Institute of Technology was established in 1861 and dedicated to the practical application of science in the arts, agriculture, manufacture and commerce; when it was opened in 1865 the courses on industrial technology dominated the whole program. The multiplication of these institutes witnessed the new orientation in industry and life. "We do not properly live in these days," one of the early Transcendentalists, J. S. Dwight, had written, "but everywhere, with patent inventions and complex arrangements, are getting ready to live. The end is lost in the means, life is smothered in appliances." The Gilded Age accepted these facts with complacence: business was the only activity it respected; comfort was the only result it sought. Gone were the tragic doubts that had vexed the Transcendentalist and made life interesting and terrible and very beautiful for all the sensitive minds: the steel mill, the mine, the counting house, claimed them; or if not that, they went to an equally materialist post-war Germany, dominated by Bismarck and Krupp, and specialized in their *Fach,* as they might specialize in railroad securities or foreign markets.

One sees the great breach between the two generations in the biographies of fathers and children, in Henry James the elder and his two sons, or, more drastically, in Bronson Alcott and his far more famous daughter Louisa. Alcott, a son of a small Connecticut farmer, got an education peddling "notions" in the plantations of Virginia; and he became both a significant personality, and within the province of education, an interesting thinker: in an age that found Spencer too mystical and difficult, he was a walking embodiment of Plato and Plotinus. Louisa, one of his children, grew up in Bronson's household, worshiped Emerson, and looked upon her father as a well-meaning but silly old man. As a result, the daughter of the philosopher reverted on a lower level to the Yankee peddler: she became a hack writer, purveying lollypops and chocolate cordials to the middle-class market. Her realistic judgment and her bitter, merciless tongue were at the service of a childish fantasy: her fiction took the place in politer circles of the new ten-cent shocker.

Of all Louisa Alcott's books only one has survived for us. It is that which was made possible by the poor and abstemious life her father's silly ways had thrust upon his children in Concord. Little Women was the picture of a happy childhood: that was all: yet it contained so much of what every child had gone through, and so much of what a starved childhood would hope for, that it became universal. Louisa's imagination offered her nothing that she could pit against this memory: with all its scrimping and penury, the reality had been equal to the heart's desire. All America after the war turned to Little Women: and why? Was it not because the only meaning of their life had been in childhood? Maturity had nothing to offer them; it was only before they had started to make a living that they had lived. Boyhood meant home: maturity meant, not a larger home, but exile. Observe that the beam cast by Transcendentalism into the generation that followed was neither Nature nor the Duty of Civil Disobedience nor the Orphic Sayings: no, Transcendentalism said nothing—except that childhood could be happy. That was a recollection that smarted!

Those who were born after 1850 scarcely knew what they were missing; but those who had reached their nonage a little before the great conflict knew it only too well. "How surprised," wrote one of them, "would some of those [Dial] writers be, if they should now in prosaic days read what they then wrote under the spell of that fine frenzy!" "We have found," wrote another, " 'realizing the ideal,' to be impracticable in proportion as the ideal is raised high. But 'idealizing the real,' as I shall maintain, is not only practicable but the main secret of the art of living. . . . There is a wise sentence in the otherwise trifling opera of the 'Grand Duchess' which says, 'If we can't get what we set our hearts on, we must set our hearts on what we can get.' " Excellent worldly wisdom! Doubtless it made one a little more comfortable as one tossed uneasily on one's bed at night, haunted by the ghost of what one might have been.

The post-war generation idealized the real, in its novels, which depicted so much of actual existence as might comfortably be exposed, and in its philosophy, which disclosed so much of the universe as could be assimilated to its feeble desires. As for those who knew better than this, what blighted fig-

ures they were—outcasts, almost beyond the pale of humanity,
the sad, grim Melville, the proud macabre Bierce. They lived
in houses that were dingy wells of darkness; and in the innermost rooms of these houses, cut off from the light in front and
the light in the rear, their souls dwelt too, unused to either
happy memories or good prospects. "Perhaps you know," wrote
Lanier to Bayard Taylor, "that with us of the younger generation in the South since the war, pretty much the whole of life
has been merely not dying." That held for the North as well.
A good part of their life was merely not dying. Each of the
principal literary figures of post-bellum America, Mark Twain,
Ambrose Bierce, Henry James, William Dean Howells, William
James, was the remains of a man. None was quite able to fill
his own shape. They might doubt that a Golden Day had once
dawned; but they had only to look around to discover the Gilt
of their own. Well might the heroine of Henry Adams's Democracy say: "You grow six inches tall and then you stop. Why
will not somebody grow to be a tree and cast a shadow?"

II

In America's Coming of Age, Mr. Van Wyck Brooks first
called attention to the broken rhythm of American life, with its
highbrows and lowbrows, its Edwardses and Franklins, its transcendentalists and empiricists. The gap between them widened
after the Civil War; for the war left behind a barbarized population which had probably lost more civil habits in four years
than the pioneer had in the course of forty. All that was left
of Transcendentalism in the Gilded Age was what Howells
showed in the hero of A Hazard of New Fortunes—"an inner
elegance." The surviving idealist did not, perhaps, particularly believe in the practical work he found himself doing; but
he did not believe in anything else sufficiently to cease doing it.
In a quite simple and literal sense, he lacked the courage of
his convictions: what was even worse, perhaps, was that he
never acquired any new convictions that might have given him
courage. The post-war generation shows us nature-lovers like
John Burroughs but no Thoreaus, schoolmasters like Sanborn
and William Harris, but no Alcotts, novelists like Howells, but

no Melvilles. It is not hard to define the difference; to put it crudely, the guts of idealism were gone.

The mission of creative thought is to gather into it all the living sources of its day, all that is vital in the practical life, all that is intelligible in science, all that is relevant in the social heritage and, recasting these things into new forms and symbols, to react upon the blind drift of convention and habit and routine. Life flourishes only in this alternating rhythm of dream and deed: when one appears without the other, we can look forward to a shrinkage, a lapse, a devitalization. Idealism is a bad name for this mission; it is just as correct to call it realism; since it is part of the natural history of the human mind. What is valid in idealism is the belief in this process of re-molding, re-forming, re-creating, and so humanizing the rough chaos of existence. That belief had vanished: it no longer seemed a genuine possibility. As Moncure Conway had said: we must idealize the real. There was the work of a Howells, a Clemens, a James. It was an act of grand acquiescence. Transcendentalism, as Emerson caustically said, had resulted in a headache; but the pragmatism that followed it was a paralysis. This generation had lost the power of choice; it bowed to the inevitable; it swam with the tide; and it went as far as the tide would carry it. When Edward Bellamy came to express the utmost of its ambitions, in the utopia called Looking Backward, his mind dwelt lovingly on telephonic broadcasting, upon perfect public restaurants, and upon purchase by sample, as in the mail-order houses—all excellent devices, perhaps, but not in themselves sufficient to stir the mind out of its sluggish acceptance of the blind drift of things. One remembers that a little earlier than Bellamy a certain Danish bishop began to institute the coöperative commonwealth by reviving the folk-ballads of his countrymen.

III

William Dean Howells was, I think, the most pathetic figure in this post-war gallery; he so narrowly missed out. If only he had not been so full of the bourgeois proprieties, if only he had not been so conscious of the smug audience he was writing for; if only he had not looked so conscientiously for the smiling side of life, which he thought of as particularly American. Could any one read Melville or Hawthorne and think that this was the characteristic touch of the American imagination? Impossible. The smile that Howells tried to preserve, undimmed by tears, undistorted by passionate emotion, was only the inane mask of the booster. One is all the more moved to pity for Howells because, believing in Tolstoi, he did not really love the America whose sensibilities he so carefully protected: he appreciated its snobbery, its pettiness, and its cruelty towards its financial inferiors. But social good will was in Howells' scheme the principal, the standard virtue: he could not see that outright animosity might be preferable, if it led to beauties and excellences that mere good will neglected to achieve.

Howells' characters were all life-sized, medium, unheroic; he painted no heroes, because he did not see them in life. Alas! that was the best reason in the world for painting them. Life exists in the possible as well as in the actual: the must and the maybe are equally valid. The conscientious littleness of Howells was painful: a man who saw as much as he did should not lean on a gentlemanly walking stick. Mixing his love with prudence, Howells never went beyond the limits of conventional society: he could admire Tolstoi but he was incapable of his splendid and terrible folly. Howells had—to a degree that should win for him forever the encomiums of our academic critics—the inner check. The inner elegance and the inner check were complementary parts of his own personality; and as a result, even the best of his novels, The Rise of Silas Lapham, never quite reaches the marrow; for these checks and these elegances were the marks of the spiritual castration which almost all his contemporaries had undergone.

Howells' failure, at bottom, was a refusal of the imagination, not of the intellect. His traveller from Altruria saw all the absurdities and hypocrisies and degradations of American life; but he saw them, as it were, only through a single organ, the eye; and in order to show their inadequacy, Howells was driven to comparing them with the practices of a quite mythical commonwealth. The point was not, however, that the

American of the Gilded Age had fallen short of some imagined human excellence: the point was that he had not succeeded in establishing a merely human life. It was this perception that later enabled Mr. Sinclair Lewis to turn Howells' disgust for the contemporary scene into sharp satire, with an imaginative reality that is entirely lacking in A Traveller from Altruria and Through the Eye of The Needle. Mr. Howells kept his kindly feelings for Silas Lapham in one department; and his contempt for the abject and futile society the Laphams were creating in another; the result is that the fall of Silas Lapham was not a tragedy, since it was too petty and personal in scope, and the picture of capitalistic America was not an inescapable satire, just for lack of some such fully-fleshed figure as Babbitt to replace Howells' mannikins. Howells' imagination and his conscience did not work together: his figures all lack that imaginative distortion which takes place when a deep emotion or a strong feeling plays upon some actuality, like a blow-torch on metal, and enables the mind to twist the thing before it into a new shape. Babbitt is quite as human a figure as Silas Lapham; but he is actualized into something more than his apparent humanity by Mr. Lewis's contempt for the banalities of his existence. The fact that Howells' technical gifts were superior to Mr. Lewis's only heightens his essential failure as an artist, and enables us to see how tightly he hugged the limitations of the contemporary scene, and recorded them in his fiction.

In contrast to Howells' blind acceptance of middle class America, Mark Twain's rebellion, in the person of Huckleberry Finn, and his eventual pessimism, may seem to carry with them a more robust flavor of reality. But as a matter of fact, Mark Twain was caught as deeply in the net of the industrialist and the pioneer as any of his contemporaries; and if he gloried in being captured, he suffered, too, from its consequences. All that was durable in Mark Twain's work traced back directly to his boyhood and young manhood on the Mississippi before the Civil War: his life as a pilot had given him his one and only glimpse of the aristocratic man—the man who uniquely knows his business, as the old pilots knew the shoals of the Mississippi

by the play of light or wind on the waters—the man who carries his point in the face of the crowd, as the Colonel defied the
scurvy mob in Huckleberry Finn. In his mastery of pilotage,
Mark Twain found himself; but he never sounded his own bottom so well in later life as he did in his career before the war.
Mark Twain did not carry his sense of aristocracy to Europe
with him; and when he refused to be "taken in" by the art gal-
leries or cities of Europe, he was just as gullible in his refusal
as were the new American millionaires, in their eager acceptance of bogus Rembrandts or Correggios.

Mark Twain's pessimism was as sentimental as Howells' optimism. Like his contempt for Europe, his contempt for mankind at large rested upon the unconscious cheapening of
values which had resulted in the miserable struggle for existence that took place in a Missouri pioneer village, or a Nevada
mining camp. Mark Twain at first saved himself from the impressions made by the blackguards and rowdies he had been
among in the Far West by taking as his ideal their more civil
counterparts, the industrialist and the inventor: these types became his creators: they alone were the people who furnished
life with an amplitude of meaning, and because of their works,
the Nineteenth Century was the "plainest and sturdiest and infinitely greatest and worthiest of all the centuries the world has
seen." But at the bottom of his soul, Mark Twain was revolted
at the spectacle: he transferred his loathing of the current brutalities to a Celtie twilight, whilst his memory transformed the
masculine smut of the roughneck into the youthful self-con-
scious dirtiness of 1601. He did not see that his Yankee mechanic was as absurd as Arthur himself, and that for every folly
or vice or imbecility that may have existed in Europe, a hundred others were springing up in post-bellum America. Mark
Twain had an eye for the wretchedness of the peasant's hovel:
but apparently he had never walked half a mile eastward from
his Fifth Avenue residence to contemplate the black squalor of
the new immigrant workers. No: for Mark Twain industrialism was an end-in-itself; and to fail to take it seriously and
magniloquently was to rob life of its chief felicities. As
M. Regis Michaud has not unjustly said, in effect, comfort was

for Mark Twain the chief art of his period. Comfort put one in a mood to pardon anything that might accompany the system which produced it!

Mark Twain's naïve worship of the paleotechnic age was summed up in the classic, the marvelous, the incredible letter he wrote to Walt Whitman in behalf of a little committee of literary men on Walt's seventieth birthday. It was written with an embarrassed avoidance of direct reference which makes one wonder a little whether Mark Twain had ever read Whitman; and it puts, better than any special explanation, the perfect fatuity of the Gilded Age. Here it is:

To Walt Whitman:

You have lived just the seventy years which are greatest in the world's history and richest in benefit and advancement to its peoples. These seventy years have done much more to widen the interval between man and the other animals than was accomplished by any of the five centuries which preceded them.

What great births you have witnessed! The steam press, the steamship, the steelship, the railroad, the perfect cotton gin, the telegraph, the phonograph, photogravure, the electrotype, the gaslight, the electric light, the sewing machine and the amazing, infinitely varied and innumerable products of coal tar, those latest and strangest marvels of a marvellous age. And you have seen even greater births than these; for you have seen the application of anesthesia to surgery-practice, whereby the ancient dominion of pain, which began with the first created life, came to an end on this earth forever, you have seen the slave set free, you have seen monarchy banished from France and reduced in England to a machine which makes an imposing show of diligence and attention to business, but isn't connected with the works. Yes, you have indeed seen much— but tarry for a while, for the greatest is yet to come. Wait thirty years, and *then* look out over the earth! You shall see marvels upon marvels added to those whose nativity you have witnessed; and conspicuous above them you shall see their formidable Result—man at almost his full stature at last!—and

still growing, visibly growing while you look. . . . Wait till
you see that great figure appear, and catch the far glint of the
sun upon his banner; then you may depart satisfied, as know-
ing you have seen him for whom the earth was made, and that
he will proclaim that human wheat is more than human tares,
and proceed to organize human values on that basis.

Mark Twain.

The thirty years duly passed: the marvels came—aeroplanes
and dirigibles that assailed helpless cities; flame throwers and
poison gases that suggested newer and more ingenious forms of
torture than rack, wheel, or faggot; explosives and deadlier
gases that threatened to exterminate not merely active combat-
ants but every vestige of organic life in the region subjected to
them. Towards the end of those thirty beautiful years, men applied, in a black rage of warfare, more satanic ingenuities than
Mark Twain himself had dreamed of when he rigged up the de-
fense which the Connecticut Yankee made against the feudal
hordes in the last chapter, and slew ten thousand men by a
bolt of electric current. Man almost at his full stature at last!
That the saturnine commentary on this letter should have come
so punctually within the allotted generation is no doubt only
an accident; but that Mark Twain should have dwelt on all
these physical improvements, and never once have thought to
mention that the Nineteenth Century was the century of
Goethe, Emerson, Tolstoi, and above all, of Whitman himself—
that, I am afraid, was no accident, but the result of his fundamental barbarism. Poor Dante! Poor Shakespeare: thrice happy
Whitman! Alas! of all the jokes Mark Twain ever labored to
utter, this that fell so innocently from his pen was perhaps the
wryest, and I am not sure but that it may cling longest to his
memory.

IV

In a different fashion from Howells, Mark Twain was afraid
of his imagination. Almost every time he felt an impulse towards poetry or beauty, he caught himself up short and mocked
at it—and this mockery, this sudden passage from the sublime

to the grotesque, became one of the stock ingredients of his humor. What did he sacrifice these fine impulses to? Nothing better than the accepted interests and habits of the utilitarian: he abruptly forgets the beauties of the Mississippi to tell the reader how many new factories have been started in Memphis, or he turns aside from the spectacle of the Hawaiian landscape to record the price of a canoe ride, or the difficulties of hiring a horse. Mark Twain's works were as full of scrappy information as an almanac: almost any externality interested him more than ⊿is own feelings, his own reactions, or the products of his imagination. In the experience of the mining community, the only uses of the imagination had been to tell tall lies: Mark Twain knew that use and employed it well in his many comic and admirable anecdotes: but he was not aware that the imagination might tell even taller truths, and at the faintest exhibition of this office, he would draw up quickly with a sudden grimace of embarrassment.

The futility of a society that denied, starved, frustrated its imaginative life, and had sacrificed every legitimate human desire for the spread of mechanical contrivances and the successes of finance, as Mark Twain himself was ready to sacrifice on occasion his most intimate convictions and do "not a bad thing, but not the *best* thing," in order to make himself more acceptable to his fellow-countrymen—this futility translated itself in Mark Twain's mind into the futility of mankind itself. In an established society, the solitary individual is always buoyed up in his weak moments by the traditions of his college, his profession, his family, his city: he feels the continuity of these institutions, knows that they have had good and happy moments; and looks forward to the time when they may come again. Pioneer society, having no past, and no continuity, could have no future, either. Men were corrupt: every man had his price: they were foolish: every one practiced his folly. Mark Twain had no notion that the pioneer settlement or the slick industrial town was a special and temporary phenomenon, something that had followed the breakdown of a great culture; and no more representative of a truly human society than the weeds that break into a garden which has fallen away from cultivation. The point is that hu-

man culture is a continuous process of choosing, selecting, nur-
turing, a process also of cutting down and exterminating those
merely hardy and fecund weeds which have no value except
their own rank life. "Choosing is creating, hear that, ye creating
ones!" Thus spake Zarathustra.

Without persistently keeping to this process, human society
tends to run wild, and in its feral state it serves no purpose
whatever, and is empty, meaningless, unattractive. Cultivation
is man's natural and proper condition; for life in the raw is
empty. Like all his generation, Mark Twain was incapable of
active choice. He accepted the values that surrounded him, and
since they were not central human values—and he was too honest not to realize this—he stored up, secretly, the bile of despair.
Man was an automaton: a mere creature of the forces that
worked upon him. That he had also been a creator, and might
be so once again—Mark Twain could not believe this. When he
exercized his aristocratic capacities for standing alone, it was on
minor and safe matters, like Christian Science and Foreign Mis-
sions. An automaton should not risk his mechanism on more
precious human issues.

The depth of Mark Twain's despair was partly hidden by
his humor; but in his contemporary, Ambrose Bierce, the mechanism of concealment was lacking, and all that one faced was
the pitted earth, iridescent with the decay of dead bodies, like
sullied black opals. Bierce's stories of the Civil War and his
other tales of horror, were all filled with an honest and irre-
deemable blackness. He, too, had seen the very worst of mankind, on the battlefield and in the pioneer town; and all the
horror of these grisly images remained with him, and colored
his imaginative life. The potion Bierce brewed was too bitter
for his contemporaries to swallow; and his work remained in
relative obscurity, which perhaps only increased his sense of
aloof contempt: Bierce's readers preferred a sentimental realist
like Bret Harte, whose local color was of the boughten kind.
Bierce did not conceal his poisons: one drank them neat: and
though they have an independent value as literature, in certain
moods, one thinks of them here as an emblem of the dismal vacancy left in the mind by the devastation of the Civil War and

the period of sordid peace that followed it. Bierce's qualities, unlike Poe's, were only partly temperamental: they arose out of an external experience which had no internal state to correspond with it outside the madhouse.

Warfare is in more than one sense a killing matter; and as the pioneer, on the testimony of John Hay, was usually old and gray before his time, so this generation of Clemens and Bierce, which had known both warfare and pioneering, and precious little of anything else, found themselves living in the shades of the charnel house. Thinking of the works and thoughts of these men, one wonders more and more what Howells meant when he said that the typical aspects of American life were the smiling ones. Was the pioneer happy? Was the returned soldier happy? Was the defeated idealist happy? And what of the industrialists who turned manufacturing into a form of warfare, surrounded their steel works or pit-heads with barbed wire, and hired armed thugs to defend their plants against strikers—were they or their workmen in a smiling mood? The open corruption of Grant's administration, equaled only by that of the lamented administration which followed the recent Great War, the graft of Tweed rings and similar organizations in every large city, the ugliness and filth of the growing industrial towns—all these things formed a villainous pattern for the mind to follow.

Men like Charles Eliot Norton, the friend of Ruskin, might be unhappy when they contemplated the scene; but at least, they did not believe that the Nineteenth was the greatest of centuries; and they did not fancy that the followers of Watt and Smiles were the highest types of humanity the earth had known. But what of people who *did* believe in the triumphs of the land-pioneer and the industry-pioneer: what of those who thought these were the Coming Men, and their works the final glory of Progress? They might quote statistics till the cows came home: they had only to look around them to discover that, humanly speaking, they were in the midst of a dirty mess. Machines got on: real estate went up: inventions became more ingenious: money multiplied: physical comforts increased: all these achievements could not be denied. But men and women—they some-

how did not reflect these great triumphs by an equivalent gain
of beauty and wisdom. On the contrary, the nervous, irritable,
scarred faces of Thomas Eakins' portraits cannot be placed
alongside the strong, reposed heads, sound even if a little fatu-
ous, that stretched between Copley and Morse; and beside the
light that shone transparently in Emerson's eye, or the great
sweet sanity of Whitman's body, or the wiry grace of Thoreau,
the noblest figures of the Gilded Age sagged and twitched a little. These children of industrialism were not the kind to keep
cool and composed before a million universes: they lost their
balance and their integrity before much less important things
than a universe.

The Gilded Age tarnished quickly: culture could not flourish in that environment. Those who could not accept their external milieu fled abroad, like Henry James. As for those who
remained, perhaps the most significant of all was William
James. He gave this attitude of compromise and acquiescence a
name: he called it pragmatism: and the name stands not
merely for his own philosophy, but for something in which
that philosophy was deeply if unconsciously entangled, the spirit
of a whole age.

v

William James, born in 1842, became a philosopher by a long,
circuitous route, which began with chemistry, physiology, and
medicine, and first flourished in its own right only as the century came to an end. As a youth, he debated over his capacities
as an artist, and threw them aside. As a mature mind, he was
ridden by an overwhelming interest in philosophy; but for
twenty years or more he threw that aside, too. The deflection of
his career from his innermost wishes was, one is inclined to
think, the outcome of a neurotic conflict, which plagued him as
a young man of twenty-eight. Equipped with a cosmopolitan
education, and a wide variety of contacts in Europe, James returned to his own soil with the wan longing of an exile. Every
time he greeted Europe, apparently, its charms increased his
homesickness. He had for America some of the agitated enthu-
siasm and unguarded receptivity of a convert. He resisted Eu-

rope: he accepted America, and though he disliked at times the dusty, meeting-house air of Cambridge, he returned to it, and breathed it, as if it had descended from the mountain tops.

One searches James's pages in vain for a *Weltanschauung:* but one gets an excellent view of America. He had the notion that pragmatism would effect an overturn in philosophy: but the fact was that it killed only what was already dead, the dry, unrelated rationalism of the theologists, or the vacant absolutism of idealists who chose to take the philosophy of Hegel without the concrete history which gave it a rational content. James's lack of a world view was due as much as anything, perhaps, to his positive dread of the difficulties of attaining one. In the crisis of his illness in 1870, under the influence of his newly attained belief in free-will, he wrote: "Not in maxims, not in Anschauungen, but in accumulated *acts* of thought lies salvation." Hence the fragmentary quality of James's philosophy. His supreme act of thought was his Psychology, a book over which he labored for a decade; but though the book is full of discreet wisdom and penetrating observation, carried to the limits of the scientific investigation of his day, James himself was dissatisfied with this act—it had impeded his progress towards Philosophy!

Beside the richness of Emerson's thought, which played over the whole field of existence, James was singularly jejune: he made up for his lack of comprehensive ideas by the brilliance and the whimsical reasonableness of his personality. He divested philosophy of its high hat and its painful white collar, and by the mere force of his presence made it human again. His personality had the curious effect of giving vitality to even moribund ideas; and the superficial reader might easily mix up the full-blooded James with the notions that lived again through this temporary transfusion. He was above all things the psychologist, commenting upon the place of philosophy and religion in the individual life, rather than the thinker, creating the philosophy which should take the place. His pragmatism was—was it not?—an attempt to cut through a personal dilemma and still preserve logical consistency: he wished to retain some surviving representative of the God of his fathers,

without throwing over the scientific method in the fields where
it had proved valuable. He used philosophy to seek peace,
rather than understanding, forgetful of the fact that if peace
is all one needs, ale can do more "than Milton can, to justify
God's ways to man." I am not sure but that this search for anesthetics may prove in the long run to be the clue to the Nineteenth Century, in all its depauperate phases. The use of ether
itself first came as a parlor sport in dull little American communities that had no good wine to bring a milder oblivion from
their boredom; and perhaps one may look upon anesthetics in
all their physical and spiritual forms—ether, Christian Science,
speed—as the culmination of the Protestant attack upon the
senses. I throw this out by the way. The fact is that pragmatism *was* a blessed anesthetic.

If one could reconstruct New England in Emerson, one could,
I think, recover great tracts of pioneer and industrial America
from the pragmatists, the pioneer especially in James, the industrialist in his great pupil, Dewey. James's insistence upon the
importance of novelty and freshness echoes on a philosophic
plane the words of Mark Twain. "What is it that confers the
noblest delight? . . . Discovery! To know that you are walking
where no others have walked, that you are beholding what human eye has not seen before; that you are breathing virgin atmosphere. To give birth to an idea—to discover a great
thought. . . . To find a new planet, to invent a new hinge, to
find the way to make the lightning carry your message. To be
the *first*—that is the idea." James's opposition to a block universe, his notion that salvation had to be worked out, his feeling
that there was no savor, no excitement, no interest "in following
the good path if we do not feel that evil is also possible and natural, nay, threatening and imminent"—what was all this, too,
but the animus of the pioneer, translated into dialectic?

I do not say this to belittle James's interest in these notions:
a philosophy must, plainly, grow out of an experience of life,
and the feeling of boundless possibility that springs from James's
pages was one of the healthy influences of the frontier. The
point is, however, that a valuable philosophy must take into account a greater range of experiences than the dominating ones

of a single generation; it is good to include these, but if it includes only these, it is still in a state of cultural adolescence. It is the remote and the missing that the philosopher must be ready to supply: the Spartan element in Plato's Republic was not familiar or genial to the Athenian temperament; but in the dry-rot of Athenian democracy it was the one element that might have restored it, and Plato went outside his familiar ground to take account of it and supply it. In Europe, James's influence has proved, I think, invigorating; for European philosophy had assimilated no such experiences as the frontier offered, and the pluralism and free-mindedness of James provided a release from a too cut-and-dried universe of discourse.

In America, however, James was only warming over again in philosophy the hash of everyday experience in the Gilded Age: he did not make a fresh combination, or a new application of these experiences; he was the reporter, rather than the creator. James's most important contribution to metaphysics was possibly his technical analysis of radical empiricism, which put relations and abstract qualities on the same plane as physical objects or the so-called external world: both were given in experience. But the totality of James's philosophy has to-day chiefly an illustrative value: woe to the seeker who tries to live by it, or find in it the key to a reasonable existence. The new ideas that James achieved were not so influential as those he accepted and rested upon; and the latter, pretty plainly, were the protestantism, the individualism, the scientific distrust of "values," which had come down in unbroken succession from Calvin and Luther, from Locke and Hobbes and Hume and Bentham and Mill.

James referred to pragmatism as "an alteration in the 'Seat of authority' that reminds one of the protestant reformation. And as, to papal minds, protestantism has often seemed a mere mess of anarchy and confusion, such, no doubt, will pragmatism seem to ultra-rationalist minds in philosophy. . . . But life wags on all the same, and compasses its ends, in protestant countries. I venture to think that philosophic protestantism will compass a not dissimilar prosperity." How curious was James's illusion that life was compassing its ends! That was just the point: that was what any one with a sense of history was forced to doubt when he contemplated the "prosperity" of Manchester, Essen, Glasgow, Lille, or Pittsburgh: life, distinctly, was not compassing its ends, and all the boasting and self-gratulation in the world could not hide the fact that something was wrong, not just in particulars, but with the whole scheme of existence. The particulars were all right in their place: men must delve and spin and weave and smelt and fetch and carry and build; but once these things get out of place, and, instead of ministering to life, limit all its functions, the ends for which life exists are not being compassed. The very words James used to recommend pragmatism should make us suspicious of its pretensions.

"For my part," cried William James, "I do not know what sweat and blood, what the tragedy of this life means except just this: if life is not a struggle in which by success, there is something gained on behalf of the universe, then it is no more than idle amusement." What is this universe which gains something by man's conflict? Is it not, perhaps, like the concept of "the country" which gains virtue by a boy scout's doing one good turn per day? The Hindu *guru*, the Platonic philosopher, aloof from this struggle, is not virtuous in James's sense; neither is the pure scientist, the Maxwell, the Faraday, the Gibbs, the Einstein—the activity of all these creatures, what is it but "idle amusement?" James's half-lost and half-redeemed universe satisfied the combative instincts: but life would still be amusing and significant were every vexatious devil banished, were every thorn plucked, were every mosquito exterminated! To find significance only in the fight, in the "action," was the signal of boredom: significant action is either the exercise of a natural function, or activity towards an end. It was the temper of James's mind, and it is the temper of protestantism generally, to take more pleasure in the obstacles than in the achievement. It has the courage to face danger and disaster: this is its great quality: but it has not the courage to face prosperity. In short, protestantism triumphs in a crisis; but it is tempted to prolong the crisis in order to perpetuate the triumph. A humane life does not demand this digging and dogging at the universe; it prospers as well in Eden as it does in the rorty wilderness outside. Growth, development, and reproduction are not categories of the battlefield.

With all the preoccupations fostered by the Gilded Age, which were handed down to the succeeding generation, it was inevitable, I think, that James's ideas should have been caricatured. His doctrine of the verification of judgment, as something involved in the continuous process of thinking, instead of a pre-existent correspondence between truth and reality, was distorted in controversy into a belief in the gospel of getting on. The carefully limited area he left to religious belief in The Will-to-Believe was transformed by ever-so-witty colleagues into the Will-to-make-believe. His conscious philosophy of pragmatism, which sought to ease one of the mighty, recurrent dilemmas of his personal life, was translated into a belief in the supremacy of cash-values and practical results; and the man who was perhaps one of the most cosmopolitan and cultivated minds of his generation was treated at times as if he were a provincial writer of newspaper platitudes, full of the gospel of smile.

On the surface, these reactions betrayed little more than the ingrained bias of James's academic colleagues; and yet, as I say, the caricature was almost inevitable, and in his persistent use of financial metaphors he was himself not a little responsible for it. James's thought was permeated with the smell of the Gilded Age: one feels in it the compromises, the evasions, the desire for a comfortable resting place. Getting on was certainly never in James's mind, and cash values did not engross even his passing attention; but, given his milieu, they were what his words reenforced in the habits of the people who gave themselves over to his philosophy. Personally, he was "against all big organizations as such, national ones first and foremost; and against all big successes and big results;" but there was nothing in his philosophy that necessitated these beliefs in his followers.

An English friend of mine used to say that the old-fashioned London banker was often, like Lord Avebury, a financier and a cultivated man: the second generation usually remained good financiers, but had no interest in art or science; the third generation were complete duffers, and good for neither activity.

Something like this happened with the pragmatists. There is an enormous distance between William James and the modern professors who become employees in advertising agencies, or bond salesmen, or publicity experts, without any sense of professional degradation; but the line that connects them is a fairly clear one. Of James one may say with sorrow that he built much worse than he knew. There was still in his personality a touch of an older and honester America—the America of Emerson and of Henry James, Senior, the America that had overthrown the old aristocracies so that every man might claim his place as an aristocrat. But the generation for whom James wrote lived in the dregs of the Gilded Age; and it was not these remoter flavors of personality that they enjoyed. As one comes to James to-day, one is touched by the spectacle of a fine personality, clipped and halted in its flight. As for his philosophy, one cannot doubt that it worked. What one doubts is whether the results of this work were valuable.

VI

It was those who stood outside the circle of the Gilded Age that have, within the last ten or fifteen years, come to seem more important than the dominating figures: Albert Pinkham Ryder in painting, Emily Dickinson in poetry, and Charles Peirce in philosophy. The overtones of the pioneering experience or the industrial scramble were absent for the most part in Peirce's writings; it was for that reason, quite as much as for their technical precision, that they remained unpopular. Peirce was not disrupted by the compromises and shifts of the Gilded Age: he lived his own life, and made none. As a philosopher, he thought deeply about logic, science, history, and the values that ennoble life; and his philosophy was what his own age deeply needed. It has remained for Professor Morris Cohen, in our own time, to resurrect his papers and to discover how fresh and appropriate they are, almost two generations after the first of them was published. Peirce had no part in the pragmatic acquiescence. His voice was a lonely protest. He was lost between two circles: the pragmatists, who were dominated, in Mr. Santayana's excellent phrase, by the foreground; and another group, equally pragmatic, equally a product of the Gilded Age, which was searching for a background. It is these latter who sought, in their own way, to fill up the vacancy that pragmatism left. William James belonged to one group; Henry James to the other; and the America after 1900 was largely the spiritual heir of one or another of these remarkable brothers.

Chapter Five   The Pillage of the Past

THE raffish vitality of the Gilded Age was not quite exhausted by manufacturing and gambling and astute corporate financiering. The pragmatists had indeed given depth to the adventure of industrialism; they had sanctioned the values that were uppermost; but they offered no clue as to what made a proper human life outside the mill of practical activity. The great captains of industry were caught within their own wheels, and were as helpless to escape as the meanest hunky who worked for them. One remembers Andrew Carnegie's resolution to resign from business in his early thirties, broaden his education, and settle down at Oxford or some other old center of culture: but the mighty wills that built the great fortunes were palsied as soon as they sought to withdraw from the game. In America, industry was not merely bread and butter; it was love, adventure, worship, art, and every sort of ideality; and to withdraw from industry was to become incapacitated for any further life.

Sooner or later, however, the reckoning was bound to come. The position had been gained; the money had been accumulated; the sons and daughters had come into leisure—well, what was to be done with it? In the Gilded Age this question concerned only a handful of people; but now that a vast accession of energies threatens the ancient economic practices, based on manual labor and personal thrift, with gradual obsolescence, the question has become a universal one, since it begins to bear on a growing army of workers, and not merely upon the minority who have escaped work altogether. The answer made by the Gilded Age is still the most popular answer in America; and for

that reason, it is perhaps not unworthy of scrutiny. The pragmatists had tried to make a culture out of a partial and one-
sided experience; those who came into leisure and money during the Gilded Age sought to achieve a culture without any
basis in experience.

Sometime during this period the epithet "predatory million-
aire" was coined. It was strictly accurate as applied to the financial activities of a Daniel Drew, a Rockefeller, a Carnegie, a
Morgan; but it was also appropriate in a wider sense. When the
time came to spend these accumulations, this generation turned
out to have a predatory notion of culture. Dissatisfied with
the dingy environment of Chicago, Pittsburgh, or New York, between 1870 and 1900, those who had the money and the special
animus began to look abroad for a cultural background. The
merely practical men were still content to get their joy out of
industrial enterprise and financial manipulation in themselves;
or they threw themselves heartily into Civil Service Reform,
cleaning up politics, the silver standard or prohibition or trust
regulation, or, with a daring sense of adventure, the initiative,
the referendum and the recall. The remnant who had lost active interest in these things, continued to pursue them in sublimated forms. Conscious of the emptiness of their lives, outside
the busy routine of trade, they sought to fill up the tedium by
spending money instead of earning it. What they had over
from sport and fashion went into art, and to the culture associated with its ancient practices.

One might think that this attempt to acquire the memorials
of culture, on the part of a Mrs. Jack Gardner or a J. Pierpont
Morgan the elder, was just the sporadic idiosyncrasy of the rich;
but the same movement was reflected in and incised into various works of the mind: in the novels of Henry James, in the historical memoirs of Henry Adams, and in the great philosophic
compendium by Mr. George Santayana which rounded off and
consummated all the more genuine aspects of this effort. Where
the pioneer had gone west, the sons of the pioneer went eastward; where the pioneer, looking upon Europe, had been an
honest boor, the new disciples of culture had become a little
servile and sheepish. At bottom, this return to Europe and this

absorption in the externalities of art, architecture, and social custom were part and parcel of the same movement: for they arose out of an uneasy sense that the old culture had gone, and a new one no longer filled the daily life. The new pioneers in Europe were not the less on the move because they were touring or sightseeing; nor were they the less interested in pecuniary goods; nor did their efforts, on the whole, produce anything more than a sense of sublime sterility. But there was this saving grace: the mind was a little more active, and with all their several incapacities, Henry James and Henry Adams and George Santayana were less subdued to banality than their counterparts among the pragmatists: a good museum has after all something that a poor society does not possess.

II

America may be defined by its possessions, or by the things that it lacks. On the second count our country is plainly a place without a long past, without a court and an aristocracy, without a stable tradition and definite connections, without the graces and souvenirs of an old and civil community. Those who feel that these deficiencies are intolerable now make what they can of the date of their ancestral arrival in the country, attempt to give the factitious aristocracy of riches the air of having long escaped from the factory or the counting house, and make up for the paucity of art in America by an exaggerated respect for the products of American craftsmanship. Sixty years ago, however, butterfly tables were still in the attic, and a good many of the "old families" had scarcely a grandfather to boast on the new soil.

The crudity and vacancy of the new American society had become apparent by the middle of the Nineteenth Century. Henry James has given his own testimony. "I saw my parents homesick, as I conceived, for the ancient order and distressed and inconvenienced by many of the more immediate features of the modern, as the modern pressed upon us, and since their theory of our better living was from an early time that we should renew the quest of the ancient on the very first possibility, I simply grew greater in the faith that somehow to manage that would constitute success in life." Henry James, Senior, was among the forerunners of the movement: the tide began to set definitely in this direction after 1870. Turning away from Nature, externalized and unassimilated, the new generation turned towards an equally foreign and externalized culture. The ugliness and sordidness of the contemporary urban scene could not be exaggerated; but they averted themselves from the scene itself, instead of confronting the forces that were producing it.

For the dominant generation of the seventies, the new personalities that had begun to humanize America did not exist: art and culture meant the past: it meant Europe: it meant over the seas and far away. Whitman was as remote as Dante: and did not Henry Adams himself, shrewdest if most pathetic of the children of light, tell of his hopeless effort to come to terms with "Concord," and the reason, too? Henry Adams "perpetually fell back into the heresy that if anything universal was unreal, it was himself and not the appearances; it was the poet and not the banker." Well might he call this heresy; for when the poet and philosopher no longer feel at the bottom of their hearts that their world is an essential part of that which surrounds them, that it is that portion of the practical life which has passed from necessity and routine into the domain of significance—when this conviction fails them, they have indeed given up the ghost. A genuine culture was beginning again to struggle upward in the seventies: A Peirce, a Shaler, a Marsh, a Gibbs, a Ryder, a Roebling, a Thomas Eakins, a Richardson, a Sullivan, an Adams, a La Farge were men that any age might proudly exhibit and make use of. But the procession of American civilization divided and walked around these men. The pragmatists became more narrow, and lived more completely in their Seventeenth Century framework; whilst those who espoused culture turned away from the living plant, pushing through the hard, argillaceous soil of the Gilded Age, in order to acquire and hold the pressed flowers, the dead and dismembered stalks, or the sweetish preserved fruits of Europe's ancient cultures—authentic because they grew in Europe, valuable, because they could not be produced in our own day, except by patent tricksters.

One does not know which was sadder, this pillage of the past, or the condition which gave rise to it. It began with an effort to be at home in Europe; the effort came into literature and took on form in the novels of Henry James. The American who loses himself in the Louvre, after having frittered away a gainful young manhood in commerce, and presently finds himself caught by a complicated and dense tissue of social custom—this figure might serve as a watermark for the general effort. James himself settled down in Europe and spent his whole life endeavoring to plumb this density. He sought to transfix in society what Whistler had so often tried to do in Nature—give a content to atmosphere and impalpability. He accepted Europe and its finish as the pioneer accepted Nature and its rawness: he did not want to do anything to it, he had no desire to assimilate it and make it over. Emerson, echoing the thoughts of every honest contemporary, had said that one could not become part of English society without wasting one's efforts in an attempt to transform it; he felt that identification would mean a loss of what was most precious in his own social heritage, and that struggle, for an outsider, would be quite futile.

Henry James, on the contrary, gave to Europe his entire loyalty; so far from wanting to change it, he wished rather to fix it: he could not be guilty of republican satire, like Meredith; he could not lift the scene to the level of tragedy, like Hardy; for James to think obliquely of Sir Willoughby Patterne's legs would have been to destroy the whole illusion of culture in which, deliberately, he enmeshed himself. Merely for an institution to be "there" was to make it, for James, valuable. What was interesting were the shades, the nice distinctions, all the evidences of long-established usage. It was not that James was altogether incapable of seeing the shallowness and tawdriness of some of his fine people; but for him these qualities were as nothing beside the fineness, the fragility of sensation, which made them so exquisitely what they were. Life might be many things in Europe; but for the classes among whom his imagination dwelt it was not raw. It had precisely what the American scene lacked: the implication of having been done a thousand times, until the finest deviation from Pattern became as violent as a complete departure. Henry James treated in his novels, in a remote gentlemanly way, the perplexities and delights that the cartoonists in Life were touching in the eighties: he answered the question: "How must one behave in Europe?"

It was useless to tell James that this acceptance of Europe as complete, final, established, was only an effort to wake the dead. What was alive in the Europe of James's day, the thought of a Tolstoi or a Nietzsche or a William Morris, had nothing to do with the Europe of place and precedent. That Europe was failing because its humanism had become dry and sterile, because what it called culture did not tend to become the shared possession of the whole community, because it was not steadily assimilating the results of commerce, science, and industry in new forms of culture, but was permitting these things to exist in the raw, and to slop over into provinces once adequately occupied by art and religion. James was no more conscious of the Europe of Nietzsche than he was of the America of Emerson: neither of these thinkers made any difference to him. As for the past, it was not a source of new life, but a final measure of what existed in the present. When one takes the past in this fashion, nothing new is good, because what is good is only what has been done before.

In short, Henry James treated Europe as a museum. By communing with its show-cases and its specimens, he could forget that the modern of Europe was precisely as inconvenient and distressing as the modern of his America. Europe's past was of course richer than America's—no thanks, however, to the forces that had been at work since the Seventeenth Century. Its valuable modern contributions were not limited to the old soil: the products of the factory and the laboratory were common to Western Civilization, and it was only in a mood of excessive self-abasement that the American need forget that from Franklin to Gibbs, from Bartram to Cope, from Fulton to Edison, the American community had continued to produce figures which could stand easily on the same pedestal as the modern European. The medieval and renaissance past had left their rich memorials in Europe, and only vestiges in America; but in those aspects of life where Western culture had become poor and mean, Europe and America were both in the same state. What people had quickly come to call the Americanization of Europe—what was that but a falling away of the old garments of culture, and the exposure of the scraggly, embryonic form of a new culture, a skeleton without flesh, and without any central organ to control and direct its random motions?

If Europe had become more conscious of its physical plight under the new regime in industry, and had raised an Owen, a Carlyle, a Marx, to denounce the conventions under which the rich became richer and the poor poorer, in the new system as well as under the old, the American was equally conscious of the fact that the old culture had become impoverished, too, and that, though it had served well in its own day, it no longer sufficed. "The New Americans . . ." said Henry Adams, "must, whether they were fit or unfit, create a world of their own, a science, a society, a philosophy, a universe, where they had not yet created a road or even learned to dig their own iron." With the living effort to create such a new world, and so carry on the work of the Golden Day, the politer heirs of the Gilded Age had nothing to do. They did not merely bury themselves, with the aid of Baedeker, in the European past: they went a step further, they began to collect and embalm its scattered fragments, with a truly Egyptian reverence for the dead.

The Eighteenth Century had in its own phase of sterility converted the curio cabinet of the country house and the loot heap of the ruling dynasty into a public museum. These new and ardent disciples of culture went a step farther: they sought, not without success, to turn the contents of the museum back again into the private house. The leader of this movement, if one can single out one figure for this distinction among a whole host of successful and wistful and pushing people, was perhaps Mrs. Jack Gardner, the builder of Fenway Court in Boston. She embodied the dream of her generation. She was in her time for "culture" what Mrs. Eddy was for "religion."

III

The dream of Mrs. Jack Gardner was fabricated slowly, according to her biographer, out of trips to Europe and a journey around the world. She was born in 1840; she thus escaped the crudities of the what-not period, when living rooms became mere albums of reminiscence, filled with picturesque memoranda in bric-a-brac. In 1873, Mrs. Gardner's biographer dutifully notes, she purchased "a small landscape," in 1875, a piece of stained glass in Nuremberg. In order to appreciate the importance of this departure, it is necessary to remember that John La Farge was beginning experiments with glass, and that Richardson was valiantly training a corps of stone-cutters, woodcarvers, painters, and sculptors during this period: after a spell of innocuous drabness, the arts were springing to life again in America: Eakins, Ryder, Blakelock, Fuller, and Homer Martin were all promising men. Mrs. Gardner was one of the first to take a decisive stand against the threat of native art in America: she turned her face abroad, and invested all her interest and energy in works of art which were, culturally, securities—which had been on the market a long time, had reached par, and could be certified by trusty advisers, like the famous critic and appraiser, Mr. Bernard Berenson.

This hunting for pictures, statues, tapestries, clothes, pieces of furniture, for the epidermis and entrails of palaces and cottages and churches, satisfied the two capital impulses of the Gilded Age: it gave full play to the acquisitive instinct, and, with the possible rise and fall of prices in even time-established securities, it had not a little of the cruder excitement of gambling in the stock-market or in real-estate. At the same time, it satisfied a starved desire for beauty and raised the pursuer an estimable step or two in the social scale. It would be hard, in fact, to find a more perfect sublimation of the dominant impulses of the time than those which Mrs. Gardner gave vent to in her search for treasures; and of course, she was not alone: I have selected her merely as a representative figure, who did with some discretion and intelligence things that untutored

Western millionaires did to their great grief—as well as the hu-
miliation of their descendants—or that titans of finance, like
Mr. J. P. Morgan, or Mr. Henry Frick did eventually on a masterly and exhaustive scale.

The essential character of all these culture-seekers was that
their heart lay in one age, and their life in another. They were
empty of the creative impulse themselves, and unwilling to nurture this impulse in the products of their own time. At best,
they were connoisseurs, who could appreciate a good thing, if
it were not too near: at worst, they were ragpickers and scav-
engers in the middens of earlier cultures. They wanted an outlet for their money: collection furnished it. They wanted
beauty: they could appreciate it in the past, or in what was remote in space, the Orient or the Near East. They wanted,
finally, to cover up the bleakness of their American heritage;
and they did that, not by cultivating more intensively what they
had, in fertile contact with present and past, but by looting
from Europe the finished objects which they lacked. Their conception of culture, and their type of financial conquest, was already perfectly expressed in the museum. The Louvre and the
British Museum, which have been the patterns of every other
great collection, are the monuments of foreign conquest: they
are the pantheons to which modern imperialisms bring back the
gods and graven images of their subjects. It was the triumph
of the American conquistadors to make the museum, filled with
the scraps of other cultures, the repository of an irrelevant and
abstract conception of culture for our own day—quite divorced
from history and common experience.

For note this: the museum in America led inevitably to the
baser sort of reproduction. There are two meanings to the word
reproduction. One has to do with the results of bringing together two different individualities which mingle and give birth
to a third, unlike either and yet akin to both. In contrast to this
is mechanical reproduction, which takes a certain pattern, and
repeats it a dozen, a hundred, a million times. Cultures flourish
in the first kind of living contact; and so far as the museum
serves this end, it exists for a worthy and rational purpose.
When an exchange of traditions, however, results only in a

mechanical reproduction, both the old culture and the new die together, for the finished products of an earlier age cannot take the place of something that must necessarily grow, change, modify itself, in constant intercourse with new desires and demands. It was in the second, mechanical sense that Mrs. Gardner and her cohorts popularized culture in America. She seized scattered objects; lugged them to Boston; and enthroned them in a building which was—one hardly knows which to call it—a home and a museum. As a home, it became a pattern for the homes of rich people in America for a whole generation; and so, at tenth hand, it became a pattern for the poorest suburban villa, with its standardized reproductions of dressers and tables and carpets. Her home in Boston could, however, scarcely be called a domestic habitation; for one had only to open the doors and place a keeper at the entrance to convert it into a splendid museum.

That is what the Gilded Age called "culture;" and this is what they dreamed of. Mrs. Jack Gardner's palace was the Platonic pattern which earlier houses anticipated, and later ones struggled bravely towards. Was it any wonder that Henry James, William James, Charles Eliot Norton, Henry Adams sat more or less obediently at her feet? She had established in Boston an atmosphere, that elusive smell of aristocratic purpose for the sake of which Henry James had clung to Europe; she had brought together in Fenway Court the things Henry Adams respectfully, learnedly, quaintly pondered in Europe; she had created something which had not existed in America before, something almost indistinguishable from the original—an original becoming a little motheaten and out-at-the-elbows—and she had done all this by the legitimated method of her age, by magnificent strokes of bounce and bargain. Was this not a happy compromise between the spiritual heirs of William and Henry James? The compromise sanctified business, because it could buy "culture," and culture—that is, past culture—was justified because it established a decent and highly reputable terminus for business. When Mr. Henry Ford restored the Wayside Inn, he was Mrs. Jack Gardner's humble and deferential disciple.

Observing all this activity from a distance, one can see that the transportation of objects of art from palaces, churches, and houses in the Old World to the homes and museums of the New was not, precisely, a creative act; but this fact does not seem to have occurred to any one during the Gilded Age; nor to have bothered any one if it did; and those who still remain fixed in the pattern of the seventies carry on this pious tradition without so much as a quiver of doubt. The dead past remained dead: the raw present remained raw; one was futile, the other was overwhelming. That culture had ever been alive, or that the human actuality had ever been more than the brutal chaos which William James so frankly accepted as the chief and undisputed ingredient of existence—well, this no one could believe. How completely these two poles of activity, the practical and the ideal, were sundered one can see best of all, perhaps, in the writings of Henry Adams. No one in his time knew better the living reality of the past, particularly of the Middle Ages in France, out of which the museums looted their separate objects; no one was more intelligently interested in the phenomena of his own day, the railroad, the corporation, the telegraph, the dynamo, the advances of mechanics and physics. Yet no one, for all his prophetic acumen, could have been more helplessly immersed in the stream of events, and unable to think himself out of them, than this quiet spectator. With all his knowledge of the past, he too succumbed to the pragmatic acquiescence.

IV

Henry Adams was a historian. Almost alone among his American contemporaries, he responded to Comte's great challenge; and sought to create out of the mere annals and chronologies and fables which had once been the stock-in-trade of the historian, a more intelligible sequence, which would lead into the future as well as the past. This attempt to achieve scientific precision did not make him forfeit his imaginative penetration of the living moments of the past. His study of Mont St. Michel and Chartres which he began at a late period of his life, after having written about current events and the political character and fate of certain periods in American history was in many ways a model of historic reconstruction: he established the mood of his period, and built into the architecture and stained glasses of the churches he examined the theology of Aquinas, the science of Roger Bacon, the songs of the troubadours, and the simple willing faith of the common people.

Since Henry Adams saw so thoroughly into the Middle Ages with its cult of the Virgin, one might fancy that he would have seen with equal insight into his own day, and the cult of the Dynamo. He was, however, so deeply immersed in his own time that he unconsciously read back into history all its preoccupations and standards. When he came to forecast the movement of history in his own day, he immediately fell into the error of location. From the standpoint of mechanical inventions, it was plain that there had been a constant acceleration of movement since, say, the Thirteenth Century. This, however, was but one activity: had Adams projected himself back into the Seventeenth Century he would have been conscious, not of space annihilating machines, but the steady increase in the art of fortification; or had he chosen painting and sculpture instead of science and machinery, he would have noted the steady decline in their relative volume and importance. The rate of change had not necessarily increased or decreased; but the departments which exhibited change had altered. That Adams should have attempted to put all these complex historic transformations into a narrow physical formula dealing with the transformation of matter and energy, shows how completely his environment had stamped him.

William James knew better than Adams on this point; and when Adams published his essay on the Phase Rule as Applied to History, James pointed out that the current theories of science as to the eventual dissipation of energies in our universe had no real bearing on human history, since from the standpoint of life what mattered was what was done with these energies before they ran down—whether the chemicals make the pigment that go into a painting, or the picric acid that annihilates a company of men in warfare. Granted that the canvas will eventually rot away, and the men will in good time die: the only significant point is what has happened in the meanwhile. Qualitatively speaking, a minute may hold as much as eternity; and for man to have existed at all may be quite as important as if he had an infinity of worlds to conquer, an infinity of knowledge to understand, and an infinity of desires to express. A hearty, an intelligent, a believing age acts from day to day on the theory that it may die to-morrow. In such periods of intensification, as in Elizabethan England, the good may well die young, because, with a complete life, death is not a frustration. Adams, though he perhaps did not realize it, was a victim of the theological notion of eternity—the notion that our present life is significant or rational only if it can be prolonged. The test of endurance is indeed an important element in providing for the continuity of generations and the stability of effort: it can be pragmatically justified: but the notion that a quantitative existence in time is a necessary measure of worth, without which life is a blank, is a notion that occurs only when life is a blank anyway.

Life, as Emerson said, is a matter of having good days. Henry Adams was discouraged: his generation had had few good days. He looked forward to the sink of energy at zero potential, or to the operation of the phase rule in history, as necessities which canceled out the pang and penalty of human efforts. If history moved inexorably from one phase to another, in the way that a solid, under suitable conditions of temperature and pressure, became a liquid, and then a gas, what mattered it that one was helpless—that one's generation was helpless? The inexorability of the law salved the laxity and the frustration. To picture a whole and healthy society, Adams's mind ran inevitably back to the past! As soon as he faced his own day, his mind jumped, as it were, off the page; and beyond predicting a catastrophe in 1917, as Western Civilization passed from a mechanical to an electrical phase, he saw nothing. In accounting for the future, he was incapable of putting desire and imagination, with their capacity for creating form, symbol, myth, and ideal, on the same level as intelligence. And intelligence itself left only a dreary prospect! The products of human culture outside science and technology became for him little better than playthings. "A man who knew only what accident had taught him in the Nineteenth Century," he wrote, "could know next to nothing, since science had got quite beyond his horizon, but one could play with the toys of childhood, including Ming porcelain, salons of painting, operas and theaters, beaux arts and Gothic architecture, theology and anarchy, in any jumble of time."

There in a brief picture was Henry Adams's generation. Its major efforts produced the grand achievements of science and technology. Science, taken as a whole, was the highest product of the time; by successive extensions into fields unknown to Bacon or Newton or Descartes, by continuous acts of thought, by the application of the scientific procedure to the earth as a whole, in geology, to organic life, in biology, and to the human community, in sociology, science was breaking outside its Seventeenth Century shell and raising problems which the logical atomism of the older thought was incapable of even expressing, much less carrying further. As a world-view, the biology of the Darwinists was still too much tainted by Calvinist metaphysics; and the loose metaphors of mechanical progress, so patent to the observers of the Nineteenth Century, were too easily substituted as patterns for the life-histories of species and societies, whilst the mechanical technique of the laboratories, placed in the dull surroundings of the paleotechnic city, tended to put to one side problems which could be solved only in the field, or by carrying the environment of the field into the laboratory. The notions of organism, of organic environment, of organic filiation had still to claim a place beside the naïve externalities of the older physics. But with all its lack of philosophic integration, the acts of thought in Nineteenth Century science made all other acts seem fairly insignificant. Science was accepted as a complete organon of life; and all its provisionally useful descriptions became finalities.

Henry Adams was far from seeing that "the great and terrible 'physical world,'" as Geddes and Branford put it, "is just a mode of the environment of Life," and that desires and ends play as important a part in the dance of life as the matter-of-fact causal descriptions which alone he respected. The truth is, Henry Adams's generation had forfeited its desires, and it was at loose ends. It treated those objects of art which are the symbols of man's desires and masteries in earlier periods tenderly, wistfully, impotently. It loved its Correggios and Tintorettos;

and its fingers lingered over velvets, brocades, and laces that happier peoples had worn; it rested in these old things, and knew that they were good. But the future had nothing to offer —except the knowledge that what is, is inevitable!

"The attempt of the American of 1900 to educate the American of 2000 must be even blinder than that of the Congressman of 1800, except so far as he had learned his ignorance . . . the forces would continue to educate and the mind would continue to react." If that were all that there was to the social process, one might well share Henry Adams's withered Calvinism. For him, the only desirable future lay in the past; what should have been a hope was a memory. If the creative impulse were not, in fact, self-renewing, if every generation did not, within its limits, have a fresh start, if all the old objects of art moldered away and nothing new ever took their places—then Adams might well read only a dreary lesson in the progress from Thirteenth Century Unity to Twentieth Century Multiplicity. Europe's spiritual capital was being spent; even those who guarded it and hoarded it could not be sure that what they called, for example, Catholicism was more than a remnant of the spirit which had once integrated every aspect of life from the marriage bed to the tomb. Steadily, Europe's fund of culture was vanishing; and its fresh acquisitions were scattered, insecure, far from covering every human activity. The American could not live long even on his most extravagant acquisitions of European culture. William James was not another Aquinas, that was plain; nor was Howells or James another Dante; and the great figures Europe still produced, an Ibsen, a Dostoyevsky, were far from getting complete sustenance from their own day; they turned away from it, rather, to folklore, philology, and the ancient institutions of religion—the dream of a Messiah, a new Christ or a newer Superman. Neither the American nor the European had more than a bare vestige of a faith or a plan of life.

> Yet we have Gods, for even our strong nerve
>   Falters before the Energy we own.
> Which shall be Master? Which of us shall serve?
>   Which wear the fetters? Which shall bear the crown?

Impotent to answer his own questions, Henry Adams was still intelligent enough to ask them. But he did not look for the answer in the only place where it may be found: he looked for it in the stars, in the annals of invention, in the credulous, mythic-materialistic past. He forgot to look for it in the human mind, which had created these idola, as it had created Moloch and Baal and Mammon; and which might turn away from its creations, as the Israelites turned away from the gods of the Philistines, once their prophets gave them a glimpse of a more organic and life-fulfilling world.

v

The criticism and completion of these two phases of American development came in the first decade of the Twentieth Century. The instrument of this criticism, Mr. George Santayana, was born in Madrid and educated in Harvard and Berlin. He brought to the American scene and its characteristic vocations an aloof inquisitiveness: the very absence of the things in America which gave contour and significance to European society redoubled their hold upon the mind of this spiritual exile: one could almost describe what was absent in America by enumerating the ideas and cultural interests that found their way into his philosophy.

What was the nature of the sense of beauty? That was a question that William James never took up again in his philosophic writings once he had silenced the urge in his private life. What was the significance of the tragic poets? That, too, was an unseemly question in a country that read Lowell and John Muir. Finally, in the Life of Reason, Mr. Santayana broke away from the two main philosophic traditions of America, the highbrow and the lowbrow, the idealist and the empiricist, and returned to those richer pastures in which Plato, Aristotle, and Lucretius had browsed. Far more successfully than William James, Mr. Santayana brought together the tender-minded and the tough-minded. He did this, not by declaring the existence of a province in which a decision must be made, not scientifically justifiable, but by giving a context to both science and idealism, or, to use the older terms, both physics and dialectics.

If he dismissed idealism as an effort to re-create the whole world, and to seize upon the entire pageant as a product of mind—of man's mind (solipsism) or of God's mind (absolutism)—he restored idealism as a mode of thinking creatively, as the mode in which art and ritual take on an independent existence and create a new home for the spirit. Thus taken, idealism is not the will-to-believe but the will-to-create: it does not lead to a respite from practical activities but to a keener and intenser struggle, in a different medium. This struggle is not inimical to science; but it does not look upon the domain of science as the entire province of human thought.

Philosophically, the pillage of the past came to an end with its consummation in the Life of Reason. It has continued as a fact, and covered wider areas, but as an idea it could go no farther: that series of volumes was a perfect exhibition of culture: it was in actuality what every other act of culture was only in vague intention—a recovery of the past, the whole past, particularly the remoter Ægean and Mediterranean past. William James said of the Life of Reason that it was grounded very deep, and would probably be looked upon as a classic by future generations: the fact that it has waited long for more than mere recognition shows the distance it went beyond the current prepossessions of the pragmatists and the culture-seekers. Mr. Santayana's thought was in a deep sense traditional; it was also, like every vital tradition, capable of bearing new fruits. In its justness of selection, its balance, its completeness, it was something that the Museums of the Gilded Age were quite unable to achieve within their own walls: it is still, however, a model of what they may reasonably aspire towards. Mr. Santayana's thoughts were not acquisitions but possessions; they were meant not merely to be exhibited but to be shared and absorbed.

In its richness of material, Mr. Santayana's philosophy had much in common with Emerson's; neither was content with an impoverished dialectic, and the academic philosophers, whose chief glory is to make bread out of straw, have frequently looked upon both thinkers as little better than amateurs and dilettantes. But, unlike Emerson, Mr. Santayana had no roots in his own day and people; and this is perhaps the source of his weakness—his vanity and his preciousness. Such roots as he had grew out of the same Boston of the nineties which created Mrs. Jack Gardner's museum. Hence Mr. Santayana's resentful attitude towards the original and the contemporary: hence, too, his complete failure of intellectual sympathy, to say nothing of an occasional loss of urbanity, in dealing with a Browning, a Whitman, a Bergson. Catholicity is something more than an arranged gesture of the mind; it must grow out of a life that is itself complete. "Could a better system prevail in our lives," Mr. Santayana once wrote, "a better order would establish itself in our thinking." Lacking such a life, yet straining after it, it is no wonder Mr. Santayana's thought bears a taint of priggishness and artful effort: it was only, as it were, by a special exercise that he was able to preserve in the affairs of the mind an attitude so foreign to his milieu and his contemporaries.

If the Life of Reason does not impel us toward a new order in our own day, it nevertheless shows clearly what the great efforts of culture produced in the past. We cannot, indeed, make the ways of other cultures our ways; but by entering into all their life in the spirit, our ways will become more deeply humanized, and will, in fresh modes, continue the living past. When we are integrated, we grow like the tree: the solid trunk of the past, and the cambium layer where life and growth take place, are unified and necessary to each other. If the pragmatists had read this lesson from history, they would not have sunk entirely into the contemporary scene; and if the pillagers of the past had realized this truth, their efforts to establish a background would not have been so superficial.

Chapter Six   The Shadow
of the Muck-rake

I

WITH the passing of the frontier in 1890, one special source of American experience dried up: the swell which between 1860 and 1890 had reached the Pacific Coast and had cast ashore its flotsam in a Mark Twain, a Bret Harte, a Muir, now retreated: the land-adventure was over. As a result, the interest in the industrial process itself intensified: the Edisons and Carnegies came to take the place in the popular imagination once occupied by Davy Crockett and Buffalo Bill. In books written for children there is a certain cultural lag which records the change of the previous generation very faithfully. The earliest children's books of the Nineteenth Century were moral tracts; they recorded the moment of Puritanism. The dime novel came in in the sixties, to echo the earliest exploits of the bad man and the outlaw; this was supplemented in the seventies by the books of Horatio Alger, written purely in the ideology of the Eighteenth Century, preaching self-help, thrift, success. In the late nineties a new set of children's books dealt with the frontiers and the Indian fights of the previous generation, to be supplanted, finally, by stories in which mechanical experiment and exploit predominated. Here is a brief revelation of our dominant idola.

With the concentration on machine industry went a similar concentration in finance. The eighties and nineties were the decades of great improvements in the steel industry, in stockyards, and in the applications of electricity; they also witnessed the first rude experiments with the internal combustion engine, which paved the way for the automobile and the aeroplane. Unfortunately, finance did not lag behind technology; and the directors of finance found methods of disposing of the unearned increment derived from land, scientific knowledge, social organization, and the common technological processes, for the benefit of the absentee owner rather than for the common welfare of the community.

The note of the period was consolidation. The great captains of industry controlled the fabrication of profits with a military discipline: they waged campaigns against their competitors which needed only the actual instruments of warfare to equal that art in ruthlessness; they erected palisades around their works; they employed private condottieri to police their establishments; they planted spies among their workers; and they viewed, doubtless with satisfaction, the building of armories in the big cities where the State Militia could be housed in times of stress to preserve "law and order." Herbert Spencer looked to industry to supplant militarism; he had not reckoned that industry itself might be militarized, any more than he had seen that warfare might eventually be mechanized; but between 1890 and 1920 all these things came to pass. The workers themselves, after various efforts to achieve solidarity in a Socialist Party or in the Knights of Labor, met the challenge by adopting a pecuniary strategy: but unlike their financial antagonists, the captains of the American Federation of Labor permitted themselves to be handicapped by jurisdictional disputes and factional jealousies; and important new industries, like oil and steel, languished without even their modicum of financial protection.

What happened in industry happened likewise in all the instrumentalities of the intellectual life. This same period witnessed the vast mechanical accretion of Columbia University and Harvard, and the establishment of Leland Stanford (railroads) and the University of Chicago (oil). Stanley Hall recorded in his autobiography, with a noble restraint, the sort of ruthlessness with which President Harper of Chicago made away with the corps of instructors and professors Hall had gathered together at Clark University: Mr. Rockefeller never got hold of oil wells and pipe lines with more adroit piracy. The concentration of publishing houses and magazines in New York was a natural accompaniment of the financial process.

This consolidation and concentration completed in industry

what the Civil War had begun in politics. The result was a pretty complete regimentation of our American cities and regions. While the process was fostered in the name of Efficiency, the name refers only to the financial returns, and not to the industrial or social method. Without doubt large efficiencies were achieved in the manufacture of monopoly profits, through special privilege, corporate consolidation, and national advertising; but the apologists for this regime were driven to express all these triumphs in the sole terms in which they were intelligible—money. In spite of its wholesale concentration upon invention and manufacture, in spite of its sacrifice of every other species of activity to utilitarian enterprise, this society did not even fulfill its own boast: it did not produce a sufficient quantity of material goods. Judged purely by its own standards, industrialism had fallen short. The one economist who devoted himself to explaining this curious failure, Mr. Thorstein Veblen, was dismissed as a mere satirist, because he showed that the actual economies of machine industry were forfeited to pecuniary aggrandizement, and through a wry standard of consumption—which confused wealth with pecuniary respectability and human vitality with keeping up appearances. For the controllers of industry, financial imperialism produced considerable profits; for the large part of the population it resulted in a bare subsistence, made psychologically tolerable by meretricious luxuries, once the sole property of a higher pecuniary caste. The Pittsburgh Survey ably documented current industrialism in every civic aspect; but it merely set down in cold print actualities which were open to any one who would take the trouble to translate bank accounts and annual incomes into their concrete equivalents.

It is no special cause for grief or wonder that the Army Intelligence tests finally rated the product of these depleted rural regions or of this standardized education, this standardized factory regime, this standardized daily routine as below the human norm in intelligence: the wonder would rather have been if any large part of the population had achieved a full human development. The pioneer, at worst, had only been a savage;

but the new American had fallen a whole abyss below this: he
was becoming an automaton. Well might Mark Twain ask in
despair, What is Man? "I have seen the granite face of Hawthorne," exclaimed Henry James, Senior, "and feel what the
new race may be!" In less than two generations that feeling
for a new human strength and dignity had been wiped out.
The popular hero of the time was that caricature of humanity,
a he-man, shrill, vituperative, platitudinous, equivocating. In
art, the memorable figures, the human ones, were caricatures:
Mr. Dooley, Potash and Perlmutter, Weber and Fields. They
alone had a shape, a flavor.

The chief imaginative expression of this period came from
men who were caught in the maw of the Middle West; and
who, whatever their background, had been fed with the spectacle of this callow yet finished civilization, the last word in mechanical contrivance, scarcely the first faint babble in culture—
sentimental yet brutal, sweet but savage. F. P. Dunne, George
Ade, Ed Howe, Hamlin Garland, Theodore Dreiser, Edgar Lee
Masters, Frank Norris, Robert Herrick—these were the writers
who caught and expressed the spirit of this interregnum; and
nearly all of these men had sprung out of the Middle West, or
had had at least a temporary resting place in Chicago during
their formative years. Jack London and Upton Sinclair belonged to this group in spirit, if not in locality. These writers
departed from the complacency of the Gilded Age, if not from
its pragmatic bias; they challenged the esoteric culture that attempted to snuggle on the ancient bosom of Europe in the
name of a coarse but upstanding vigor derived completely from
the life around them. Born between the close of the Civil War
and 1880, by the place of their birth they had inherited the
memories of the pioneer, by the time of their birth, those of
industrialism and the new immigrant. Mawkish middle-class
writers, like Meredith Nicholson and Booth Tarkington saw
this life through the genuine lace curtains of respectable par-
lors: but the more virile representatives of this period knew it
from the saloon to the stockyard, from the darkest corner of the
cellar to the top of the new skyscrapers.

II

The shadow of the muck-rake fell over this period. That was to its credit. But business went on as usual and the muck remained. Those who defended the sweating of labor, the building of slums, the bribery of legislatures, the piratical conduct of finance, the disorderly and short-sighted heaping up of very evanescent material goods were inclined to blame the muck-rake for the existence of the muck, just as they would blame the existence of labor agitators for the troubles they attempt to combat—which is very much like blaming the physician for the plague. As a result of the muck-rake, white-wash cans and deodorizing solutions came into general use: philanthropic bequests became more numerous and more socialized; social work expanded from the soup kitchens and down-and-out shelters to social settlements; and the more progressive factories even began to equip themselves with gymnasiums, lunchrooms, orchestras, and permanent nurses. If modern industrial society had in fact been in the blissful state its proponents always claimed, it would be hard indeed to account for all these remedial organizations; but in the widening of the concept of "charity" the claims of the critics, from Owen to Marx, were steadily being recognized.

Frank Norris in The Octopus and The Pit, Upton Sinclair in The Jungle, and Jack London in the numerous biographic projections he called novels, faced the brutal industrialism of the period: they documented its workings in the wheatfield, the prison, the stockyard, the stock exchange, and the vast purlieus of la ville tentaculaire; Mr. Robert Herrick, a little more restrained but just as keenly awakened, added to the picture. The work that these men accomplished could scarcely be called a spiritual catharsis; for it left the reader the same man that it found him; it was rather a regurgitation. To their credit, they confronted the life about them: they neither fled to Europe nor fancied that all American aspects were smiling ones. But these vast cities and vacant countrysides were not something that they took in and assimilated and worked over into a new pattern: it did not, in fact, occur to these writers that the imagination had an important part to play in the process. They were reporters, or, if they thought of themselves more pretentiously, social scientists; their novels were photographs, or at any rate campaign documents.

With unflinching honesty, these novelists dug into the more putrid parts of modern American society and brought to light corruption, debasement, bribery, greed and foul aims. Fight corruption! Combat greed! Reform the system! Their conclusions, implicit or expressed, could all be put in some terse admonition. They took these symptoms of a deep social maladjustment to be the disease itself; they sought to reach them by prayer and exhortation, carried on by street corner evangelists, by legislative action—or, if necessary, by a revolutionary uprising in the fashion of 1789.

Perhaps the most typical writers of this period were implicated in political programs for reform and revolution. In their reaction against the vast welter of undirected forces about them, they sought to pave the way for political changes which would alter the balance of political power, drive out the "predatory interests," and extend to industry itself the republican system of government in which the nation had been conceived. Upton Sinclair's The Industrial Republic, which followed close on his great journalistic beat, The Jungle—the smell of tainted meat, which accompanied the United States Army to Cuba, still hung in the air—was typical of what was good and what was inadequate in these programs. To Mr. Sinclair, as to Edward Bellamy some twenty years earlier, the Social Commonwealth, full-panoplied, was just behind the horizon. He was hazardous enough to predict its arrival within a decade. With Mr. Sinclair's aim to establish a more rational industrial order, in which function would supplant privilege, in which trained intelligence would take the place of inheritance, in which the welfare of the whole community would be the prime end of every economic activity, I am in hearty sympathy. What was weak in Mr. Sinclair's program was the assumption that modern industrial society possessed all the materials essential to a good social order. On this assumption, all that was necessary was a change in power and control: the Social Commonwealth would simply diffuse and extend all the existing values. These writers accepted the trust, and wanted the principle of monopoly extended: they accepted the bloated city, and wanted its subways and tenements socialized, as well as its waterworks; there were even authoritarian socialists, like Daniel De Leon, who believed that the corporate organization of workers, instead of being given added responsibility as guilds, would disappear entirely from the scene with the Socialist State. Concealed under revolutionary phrases, these critics could envisage only a bourgeois order of society, in which every one would have the comforts and conveniences of the middle classes, without the suffering, toil, anxiety, and frustration known to the unskilled worker.

What was lacking in such views was a concrete image of perfection: the "scientific" socialists distrusted utopias, and so made a utopia of the existing order. In attack, in criticism, they did able work; but when it came to offering a genuine alternative, their picture became a negative one: industry without millionaires, cities without graft, art without luxury, love without sordid calculation. They were ready to upset every aspect of modern industrial society except the fragmentary culture which had brought it into existence.

Now, were the diffusion of existing values all that was required of a better social order, the answer of capitalism was canny and logical: the existing regime could diffuse values, too. Did not bank accounts spread—and Ford cars—and movies—and higher wages in the skilled trades? What more could one want? Why risk one's neck for a Social Commonwealth when, as long as privilege was given a free hand, it would eventually provide the same things? Thus the socialist acceptance of the current order as a "necessary stage," and the socialist criticism, "Capitalism does not go far enough," have been answered by the proposition that it actually does go farther: the poor do not on the whole get poorer, but slowly march upward in the social scale.

The evils of privilege and irresponsible power in America were of course real; but the essential poverty of America was a qualitative poverty, one which cut through the divisions of rich and poor; and it has been this sort of poverty which has prevented us from projecting in the imagination a more excellent society. Life was more complicated in America but not more significant; life was richer in material goods but not in creative energies. These eager and relentless journalists were unaware of the necessity for establishing different kinds of goods than the existing ones; they had no notion of other values, other modes, other forms of activity than those practiced by the society around them. The result is that their works did not tend to lead out of the muddle. Their novels were interesting as social history; but they did not have any formative effect: for they sentimentalized the worker to the extent of always treating him as a victim, and never making out of him a hero. The only attempt to create a heroic portrait of the worker came towards the end of the muck-raking period; it was that of Beaut McGregor in Sherwood Anderson's Marching Men, a half-wrought figure in an imperfect book.

What the American worker needed in literature was discipline, confidence, heroic pictures, and large aims: what he got even from the writers who preached his emancipation was the notion that his distressing state was only the result of the capitalist's villainy and his own virtues, that the mysterious external forces of social evolution were bound eventually to lift him out of his mean and subservient condition and therefore he need not specially prepare himself to bring about this outcome —and that anyway the odds were always against him! It is doubtful whether this analysis could be called accurate science; it certainly was not high literature. For all the effect that these painstaking pictures had in lifting the worker onto a more active plane of manhood, one would willingly trade the whole literature for a handful of good songs. I am not sure but that the rowdy, impoverished lyrics of the wobblies were not more stirring and formative—and that they may last longer, too.

III

There were two writers who stood outside this gallery: Jack London, who created his own Superman, and Mr. Theodore Dreiser, who depicted the whole American scene without any propagandist bias. They do not alter the contours of the picture; they merely show how futile the will-to-power and the desire to face facts became, when pushed to their conclusions without reference to rational ends.

Jack London came to maturity in the nineties; and after a career as oyster pirate in San Francisco Bay, as a tramp with Coxey's army, as an adventurer in Alaska, after participating in all the coarse and wearing manual labor that may offer itself to a willing lad, he acquired the scraps of an education, and went in for writing, as an easier kind of livelihood. He quickly achieved popularity. He had only to tell his life over again—to make a story of it in the newspaper sense—to feed the romanticism of the big urban populations which now began to swallow the five, ten, and fifteen cent magazines. London became a sort of traveling salesman of literature, writing to his market, offering "red blood" and adventure to people who were confined to ledgers, ticker-tapes, and Sunday picnics. He brandished the epithet socialist as a description of himself and his ideas; but he was gullible enough to swallow Kipling's doctrine of the White Man's Burden, believed in the supremacy of the Nordics, who were then quaintly called Anglo-Saxons, and clung to socialism, it would seem, chiefly to give an additional luster of braggadocio and romanticism to his career; for socialism, to London's middle-class contemporaries, was an adventure more desperate than the rush for gold in the Klondike. Superficially London perhaps believed in the socialist cause; but his personal activities had scarcely the chemical trace of a public interest in them; and one need only go below the surface to see that he betrayed his socialism in all his ingrained beliefs, particularly, his belief in success, and in his conception of the Superman.

The career of the Superman in America is an instructive spectacle. He sprang, this overman, out of the pages of Emerson; it was Emerson's way of expressing the inexhaustible evolutionary possibilities of a whole race of Platos, Michelangelos, and Montaignes. Caught up by Nietzsche, and colored by the dark natural theology Darwin had inherited from Malthus, the Superman became the highest possibility of natural selection:

he served as a symbol of contrast with the coöperative or "slave morality" of Christianity. The point to notice is that in both Emerson and Nietzsche the Superman is a higher type: the mark of his genius is the completer development of his human capacities. London, like his whole generation, scarcely knew of Emerson's existence: one has only to note the way in which Frank Norris respectfully refers to "great" New England writers like Lowell and Whittier to know that he had probably not read even these minor writers. London, however, seized the suggestion of the Superman and attempted to turn it into a reality. And what did he become? Nothing less than a preposterous bully, like Larssen, the Sea-Wolf, like Burning Daylight, the miner and adventurer, like his whole gallery of brutal and brawny men—creatures blessed with nothing more than the gift of a magnificent animality, and the absence of a social code which would prevent them from inflicting this gift upon their neighbors. In short, London's Superman was little more than the infantile dream of the messenger boy or the barroom tough or the nice, respectable clerk whose muscles will never quite stand up under strain. He was the social platitude of the old West, translated into a literary epigram.

What London called "white logic," which he sought to erase by drink, was the perception that life, as he had found it, was empty. The logic was faultless; the insight was just; but as a writer and a mythmaker it remained for him to fill it up, to use the materials he had gathered as the painter uses his pigments, to create a more significant pattern. To do this he was impotent: hence his "scientific" determinism. "You made me what I am to-day: I hope you're satisfied." This, in the words of a popular ballad, was the retort of the handicapped and limited American artist to his environment. He held a mirror up to society; and to read the mind of a London or a Dreiser is to read what was passing in the streets about him; or, vice-versa, to record as in a lens the dull parade of men, women, factories, downtowns, waterfronts, suburbs, railroads, murders, lusts, connubialities, successes, chicanes, is to read their novels.

The bewildered chaos of the sons of the pioneer, as they reached their destination and recoiled into muzzy reflection, is best illustrated, I think, in the novels of Mr. Theodore Dreiser. Mr. Dreiser has a power and reach which set him well above his immediate contemporaries. Across the panorama of the mid-American prairie, where Chicago sits like the proverbial spider in the midst of her steel web, Mr. Dreiser flung his canvas; his Philadelphia, too, is spiritually part of that Chicago. Huge figures, titans of finance, who practice "art for art's sake" in the pursuit of money, or "geniuses" in art, who are business men in everything except their medium, dominate the scene; they wander about, these Cowperwoods and Witlas, like dinosaurs in the ooze of industrialism. Mr. Dreiser's books reflect this bulk and multitudinousness: they are as full of details as a day's shopping: with a vast hippopotamus yawn he swallowed the minutiæ of America's physical activities: you might find in his books the wages of laundry wagon drivers in 1894, the style of women's gloves in 1902, how one cashes a check at a bank, the interior arrangements of a modern hotel, the details of a criminal prosecution.

By what means does he handle this material? What makes it significant? There are no means; or rather, they are those of the census taker, whose schedule covers everything. There is a superficial resemblance between Dreiser and Zola; but Zola, being the product of the old and high civilization of Provence, had some conception of what a humane life might be, and not for a second was he unconscious of his purpose to criticize the church, to portray the evils of drunkenness, to expose the brutalities of the farm or the steel works: he had the advantage of describing a society that had known better days, and these days were his implicit point of reference. What can we say of Mr. Dreiser? He is simply bewildered. He is attracted to anything that exhibits size, power, sexual lust; believing in these things alone, he is critical of any institution or idea that stands in their way. His heroes know what it is to have material success and to conquer women; but their conquests lead nowhere and develop into nothing. One thing bobs up; another falls down; and in the long run none of their affairs, financial or sexual, are of any consequence. It is a picture of society: yes: but so is the Sunday newspaper.

One wonders about the curious naïveté of Mr. Dreiser's mind. He is free from conventional restraints; he has the healthy indifference of the honest physician who encounters everything in the day's work. He thinks other people ought to be free, too; and he can scarcely see that there are any consequences in sexual passion, for example, except a conflict with the formalities of the social code. The reactions of the wife of the "Genius" to his adventures with other women seem to the hero irrelevant; they are due, not to the inherent psychology of the relationship, but to her being conventionally brought up! In his callowness, in his heavy platitudes, in his superficial revolt against "morality," Mr. Dreiser was but the forerunner of a host of magazines that live on "confessions," fabricated or real, of ordinary men and women, without any more sense of direction or purpose or humane standards than Mr. Dreiser's own heroes and heroines. His novels are human documents; so is a pair of shoestrings, a torn glove, a footprint. But the chief thing they give evidence of is the total evaporation of values in the modern industrial environment, the feebleness of the protestant morality, which was all that kept the social bond from breaking entirely in the old days; and the total lack, in this crass new life, of any meanings or relationships beyond the raw fact.

Culture in its many ramifications is a working over of the raw fact. Just as eating, among civilized peoples, is not a mere hacking and gnawing at flesh and bones, but an occasion for sociability and civil ceremonies, to the extent that the ceremony frequently becomes as important as the fact itself and works out into a separate drama, so every act tends to be done, not just for its own sake, but for the social values that accompany it: the taste, the conversation, the wit, the sociability are esthetic filaments that bind men together and make life more pleasing. To the extent that these shared meanings come into existence and spread over all the details of the day's activities, a community is cultured; to the extent that they disappear, or have no place, it is barbarous. The hurried business man who snatches his lunch, snatches his girl in the same way: his lust is as quickly exhausted as his appetite; and he looks around for

a new stimulus, as he might scan the menu for a new dish. Experience of this sort tends to be truncated; it remains on the
level of the physical fact, and the physical fact becomes dull
and unimportant, and must be succeeded by new stimuli, which
eventually become stale, too. Culture, on the other hand, implies the possibilities of repetition. Like fine poetry or music,
the hundredth occasion often finds an act as interesting as the
first. If this were not so, life would be intolerable; and because
it is so, it is no wonder that the barbarians Mr. Dreiser portrays
find all their adventures stale, and all their different achievements tending towards a deadly sameness. Their lives are
empty, because lust and power are empty, so long as they do
not contrive situations in which power is turned to rational
ends and produces efficient industries, fine cities, and happy
communities—or sexual passion its friendship, its salon, its
home, its theater in which the private interest becomes sublimated and amplified into more agreeable forms of social life.

IV

Among the group of New Englanders established in Chicago
at the beginning of the century, Mr. John Dewey was perhaps
the most distinguished. Among all the writers of this milieu
and period, he expressed in his philosophy something more
than the mere welter of existence. From the beginning Mr.
Dewey was bracketed with William James as one of the founders and developers of pragmatism, or as he himself preferred to
call it, instrumentalism; but, in spite of similarities of approach,
there were differences between these men which at bottom reflected the intervening of almost a generation between the birth
of James and that of Dewey.

William James had a style. Dreiser, Dewey, the commanding
writers of the early Chicago school, were at one on this point:
they had no style: they wrote in a language which, however
concrete its objects, was as fuzzy and formless as lint. There is
a homely elegance in James's writing, a beauty in the presentation of the thought, even if the concept of beauty was absent
from his philosophy; in the earlier writing of Dewey, on the
other hand, one looks in vain for either the concept or its lit-

erary equivalent. The comedown is serious. Style is the indi-
cation of a happy mental rhythm, as a firm grip and a red cheek
are of health. Lack of style is a lack of organic connection:
Dreiser's pages are as formless as a dumpheap: Mr. Dewey's
pages are as depressing as a subway ride—they take one to one's
destination, but a little the worse for wear. Mr. Randolph
Bourne once characterized this quality of Mr. Dewey's mind as
"protective coloration;" and the phrase is accurate enough if
one means that the creature has identified himself in shape and
color with his environment. No one has plumbed the bottom
of Mr. Dewey's philosophy who does not feel in back of it the
shapelessness, the faith in the current go of things, and the general utilitarian idealism-of Chicago—the spirit which produced
the best of the early skyscrapers, the Chicago exposition, Burn-
ham's grandiose city plan, the great park and playground system, the clotted disorder of interminable slums, and the vitality of a handful of experimental schools.

Mr. Dewey's philosophy represents what is still positive and
purposeful in that limited circle of ideas in which the American
mind was originally born; he is at home in the atmosphere of
protestantism, with its emphasis upon the rôle of intelligence
in morals; in science, with its emphasis upon procedure, technique, and deliberate experiment; and he embraces technology
with the same esthetic faith that Mr. Henry Ford embraces it.
Above all, Mr. Dewey believes in democracy; that was at the
bottom of his many acceptances of the milieu; what had been
produced by the mass of men must somehow be right, and must
somehow be more significant than the interests which occupy
only a minority! In Mr. Dewey the American mind completed, as it were, its circle, and returned to its origin, amplify-
ing, by the experience of a century, the essential interests of an
Edwards, a Franklin, a Paine.

To the things that stand outside this circle of ideas, Mr.
Dewey has been essentially antagonistic, or at least unsympa-
thetic. He has been a severe and just critic of conventional
education; and he has undermined conceptions of philosophy,
art, and religion which represented merely the mummified experiences and aims of other generations: but his criticisms have

been conducted with an unqualified belief in the procedures of
common sense and technology, because these procedures have
led to practical "results." Happiness, too, for him "is found
only in success; but success means succeeding, getting forward,
moving in advance. It is an active process, not a passive outcome." That is quite another definition of happiness than the
equilibrium, the point of inner rest, which the mystic, for example, seeks; but for Mr. Dewey a less active kind of happiness
always tends to be "totally separated from renewal of the
spirit." In other words, happiness means for Mr. Dewey what
it meant for the pioneer: a preparation for something else. He
scarcely can conceive that activity may follow the mode of the
circle or the pendulum, rather than the railroad train.

In spite of all these opacities, it would be absurd to ignore
the great service that instrumentalism has performed; for it has
crystallized in philosophic form one of the great bequests of science and modern technology: the respect for coöperative thinking and for manual activity—experiment and invention—in
guiding and controlling this process. The notion that action
by itself was undignified and foreign to the life of the mind
was, of course, a leisure class superstition. Creative thought is
not a polite shuffling of observations, memories, and a priori
logic: that is but one phase of the whole process: man thinking
is not a spectatorial "mind" but a completely operative human
organism, using in various degrees and at various stages every
part of his organism, down to his viscera, and every available
form of tool, from the finger which might trace a geometrical
theorem in the sand to the logarithm table or the electric fur-
nace. The otiose, leisure-class notion of thinking is that it is
the reflection of what one reads in a book or gets by hearsay
from other people: the great achievement of the scientific
method was to supplant the scholar's chair—which does in fact
peculiarly serve one phase of the thinking-process—by the work
of the field and the laboratory, by exploration, observation, mechanical contrivance, exact measurement, and coöperative intercourse. With the introduction of the scientific method, men
began to think consciously as whole human beings: the worker,
the rambler, the traveler, the explorer, enlarged the scope of

the mind. If this movement was accompanied by some loss, per-haps, in that part of the thinking process covered by dialectics, the gain was nevertheless a great one.

Mr. Dewey seized upon this achievement and brought out its significance admirably. Its implications should not be neglected. According to Dewey, thought is not mature until it has passed into action: the falsity of philosophy is that it has frequently dealt with ideas which have no such issue, while the weakness of the practical world is that its actions are unintelligent rou-tine, the issue of an unreflective procedure. Action is not op-posed to ideas: the means are not one thing, and the final re-sult of attending to them quite another: they are not kitchen maids and parlor guests, connected only by being in the same house. Means which do not lead to significant issues are il-liberal and brutal; issues which do not take account of the means necessary to fulfill them are empty and merely "well-meaning." A transcendentalism which takes such high ground poor humanity cannot stand on it, or an empiricism which takes such low ground that it introduces no excellence into brute existence—both these things are inimical to life, and ab-surd—and it has been Mr. Dewey's great merit to point out this absurdity, and so open the way to a more complete kind of ac-tivity, in which facts and values, actualities and desires, achieve an active and organic unity.

In its flexibility, in its experimentalism, in its emphasis upon the ineptitude of any finality, except that involved in the proc-ess of living itself, with the perpetual intercourse between the organism and its implicated environment, Mr. Dewey's philoso-phy expresses a continuously formative part of our American experience. For the European, roughly speaking, history is what prevents anything new or fresh from being done. It needed the dislocation of settling a New World to discover a to-morrow not actually given in a host of yesterdays. In so far as Mr. Dewey has given expression to these things, his work has been to the good: it is not that flexibility and experiment are good in themselves: there are times when it is necessary to be as stiff as a ramrod and as dogmatic as a Scotch dominie—but these things represent a genuine addition to the European experience of life, and to introduce them as categories in philosophy is to extend its boundaries.

The deficiencies of Mr. Dewey's philosophy are the deficiencies of the American scene itself: they arise out of his too easy acceptance of the Seventeenth and Eighteenth Century framework of ideas; and although he has written about the influence of Darwinism on philosophy, and has done some of his best work in enriching the concepts of philosophy with biological illustrations and clues, he has not been sufficiently critical of the doctrines and writers whose works lean closest to his own habits of thinking. The utilitarian type of personality has been for the instrumentalist a thoroughly agreeable one: I recollect eulogies of Bacon in Mr. Dewey's works, but none of Shakespeare; appreciations of Locke, but not of Milton; of Bentham, but not Shelley and Keats and Wordsworth and Blake. The thinkers who saw social welfare as the principal object of existence, and who naïvely defined it in terms of man's control over the externalities of his environment, through the employment of science and technology, have been nearest to Mr. Dewey's heart. He has even written as if the telephone did away with the necessity for imaginative reverie—as if the imagination itself were just a weak and ineffectual substitute for the more tangible results of invention!

This aspect of Mr. Dewey's instrumentalism is bound up with a certain democratic indiscriminateness in his personal standards: a Goodyear and a Morse seem to him as high in the scale of human development as a Whitman and a Tolstoi: a rubber raincoat is perhaps a finer contribution to human life than "Wind, Rain, Speed." What indeed is his justification for art? Let him answer in his own words. "Fine art, consciously undertaken as such, is peculiarly instrumental in quality. It is a device in experimentation, carried on for the sake of education. It exists for the sake of a specialized use, use being a training of new modes of perception. The creators of such works are entitled, when successful, to the gratitude that we give to inventors of microscopes and microphones; in the end they open new objects to be observed and enjoyed." This is a fairly

back-handed eulogy, unless one remembers Mr. Dewey's intense
gratitude for all mechanical instruments.

In a similar mood, Mr. Dewey speaks of the "intrinsic worth
of invention;" but the point is, of course, that except for the
inventor, who is *ipso facto* an artist, the invention is good for
what it leads to, whereas a scene in nature, a picture, a poem,
a dance, a beautiful conception of the universe, are good for
what they are. A well-designed machine may also have the
same kind of esthetic value: but the independent joy it gives
to the keen mechanic or engineer is not the purpose of its design: whereas art has no other purpose; and when a Duchamp-
Villon or a Man Ray wants to create the esthetic equivalent of
a machine, he does not employ an engineer, but goes through
the same process he would undergo to model the figure of a
man. Esthetic enjoyment will often lead to other things, and
it is all the happier for doing this: the scene in nature may
lead to the planting of a park, the dance may promote physical
health: but the essential criterion of art is that it is good without these specific instrumental results, good as a *mode of life,*
good as a beatitude. An intelligent life, without these beati-
tudes, would still be a poor one: the fact that Bentham could
mention pushpins in the same breath as poetry shows the deeply
anesthetic and life-denying quality of the utilitarian philosophy.

There are times when Mr. Dewey seems ready to admit this
deficiency. In Reconstruction in Philosophy he was aware of
the danger of utilitarian monsters, driving hard bargains with
nature, and he was appreciative, to a degree unusual in his
thought, of the contemplative life, with its loving intercourse
with forms and shapes and symbols in their immediacy. The
weakness of Mr. Dewey's instrumentalism is a weakness of practical emphasis. He recognizes the place of the humane arts, but
his preoccupation has been with science and technology, with
instrumentalism in the narrow sense, the sense in which it occurs to Mr. Babbitt and to all his followers who practice so as-
siduously the mechanical ritual of American life. Conscious of
the weakness of the academic critic, who may take art as an abstract end-in-itself, quite divorced from life and experience, he

forgets that Mr. Babbitt treats showerbath fixtures and automobile gadgets in the same way—as if a life spent in the pursuit of these contrivances was a noble and liberal one. What
Mr. Dewey has done in part has been to bolster up and confirm
by philosophic statement tendencies which are already strong
and well-established in American life, whereas he has been apa-
thetic or diffident about things which must still be introduced
into our scheme of things if it is to become thoroughly humane
and significant. What I have said of William James applies with
considerable force to his disciple.

v

In the revulsion that followed America's entry into the war,
Randolph Bourne, one of Mr. Dewey's most ardent and tal-
ented disciples, found himself bereft of the philosophy which
had once seemed all-sufficient; its counsel of adjustment left him
rebelliously turning his back on the war-situation and the war-
technique. In his recoil, Bourne put his finger upon the shallow side of Mr. Dewey's thinking; and his criticism is all the
more adequate and pertinent because it rested on a sympathetic
understanding of the instrumentalist philosophy.

"To those of us," he wrote, "who have taken Dewey's philosophy almost as our American religion, it never occurred that
values could be subordinated to technique. We were instrumentalist, but we had our private utopias so clearly before our
minds that the means fell always into place as contributory.
And Dewey, of course, always meant his philosophy, when
taken as a philosophy of life, to start with values. But there
was always that unhappy ambiguity in his doctrine as to just
how values were created, and it became easier and easier to assume that just any growth was justified and almost any activity
valuable so long as it achieved its ends. The American, in living out his philosophy, has habitually confused results with
product, and been content with getting somewhere without ask-
ing too closely whether it was the desirable place to get. . . .
You must have your vision, and you must have your technique.
The practical effect of Dewey's philosophy has evidently been
to develop the sense of the latter at the expense of the former."

Without these superimposed values, the values that arise out of vision, instrumentalism becomes the mere apotheosis of actualities: it is all dressed up, with no place to go. Unfortunately, since the breakup of medieval culture, with such interludes as humanism and romanticism have supplied, men have subordinated the imagination to their interest in practical arrangements and expediences, or they have completely canalized the imagination itself into the practical channels of invention. This has led not alone to the conquest of the physical environment but also to the maceration of human purposes. The more men go on in this way, the farther they go from the domain of the imagination, and the more impossible it becomes for them to recognize the part that vision must play in bringing all their practical activities into a common focus. Their external determinism is only a reflection of their internal impotence: their "it must" can be translated "we can't." As Bourne said, the whole industrial world—and instrumentalism is only its highest conscious expression—has taken values for granted; and the result is that we are the victims of any chance set of values which happens to be left over from the past, or to become the fashion. We are living on fragments of the old cultures, or on abortions of the new, because the energies that should have gone into the imaginative life are balked at the source by the pervasive instrumentalism of the environment.

An instrumental philosophy which was oriented towards a whole life would begin, I think, not by a criticism of obsolete cultural values—which are already criticized by the fact that they are obsolete and inoperative and the possession of a small academic class—it would begin, rather, by a criticism of this one-sided idealization of practical contrivances. We shall not get much nearer a genuine culture by ignoring all the products of the creative imagination, or by palming off our practical instrumentalities—excellent though they are in their place—as their full equivalent. "If your ideal is to be adjustment to the situation," as Bourne well said, "in radiant coöperation with reality, then your success is likely to be just that, and no more. You never transcend anything. . . . Vision must constantly outshoot technique, opportunist efforts usually achieve even less than what obviously seemed possible. An impossibilist *élan* that appeals to desire will often carry farther. A philosophy of adjustment will not even make for adjustment."

Brave words! The pragmatists have been defeated, these last few centuries, because they have not searched for the kingdom, the power, and the glory together, but have sought to achieve power alone; so that the kingdom ceased to be a tangible one, and they knew no glory, except that which flowed out of their pursuit of power. Without vision, the pragmatists perish. And our generation, in particular, who have seen them fall back, one by one, into commercial affairs, into administrative absorption, into a pained abandonment of "reform," into taking whatever fortune thrusts into their laps, into an acquiescence even more pathetic, perhaps, than that of the disabled generation which followed the Civil War—our generation may well doubt the adequacy of their complaisant philosophy. "Things are in the saddle," Emerson said, "and ride mankind." We must overthrow the rider, before we can recover the horse: for otherwise, horse and rider may drive to the devil.

Chapter Seven   Envoi

ENTERING our own day, one finds the relations of culture and experience a little difficult to trace out. With the forces that have come over from the past, it is fairly easy to reckon: but how these are being modified or supplanted by new efforts of experience and new stores of culture one cannot with any assurance tell. Is Robert Frost the evening star of New England, or the first streak of a new dawn? Will the Dewey who is struggling to step outside his old preoccupations influence the coming generation, or will the more passive and utilitarian thinker continue to dominate? Will our daily activities center more completely in metropolises, for which the rest of the country serves merely as raw material, or will the politics and economics which produce this state give place to programs of regional development? What is the meaning of Lindsay and Sandburg and Mrs. Mary Austin? What is the promise of regional universities like Nebraska and North Carolina and New Mexico? May we look forward to a steady process of re-settlement; or will the habits of nomadry, expansion, and standardization prevail?

The notion that the forces that are now dominant will inevitably continue and grow stronger will not stand a close examination. Those who take refuge in this comfortable view are merely accepting facts as hopes when they think this would be desirable, or hopes as facts, when they profess that it is unavoidable. The effort of an age may not lead to its prolongation: it may serve to sharpen its antithesis and prepare the way for its own demise. So the stiffening of the old Renaissance motifs in the Eighteenth Century did not lead to their persistence: they formed the thorny nest in which Romanticism was hatched. It was in the decade of Watt's steam engine that Percy's Reliques were published; it was in the decade of the steamboat that Scott published his Waverley novels. Romanticism, for all its superficialities, gave men the liberty to breathe again; out of the clever imitations of Chatterton grew Wordsworth, and out of the meretricious Gothic of Walpole, Hugo and Viollet-le-Duc took possession anew of Notre Dame. I do not say that the Romantic poets changed the course of industrialism; but they altered the mood in which industrialism was received and quickened the recognition of its potentialities for evil, which a blind and complacent utilitarianism might have ignored for generations.

We have seen American culture as formed largely by two events: the breakdown of the medieval synthesis, in the centuries that preceded America's settlement and by the transferal to the new soil of an abstract and fragmentary culture, given definitive form by the Protestants of the Sixteenth Century, by the philosophers and scientists of the Seventeenth, and by the political thinkers of the Eighteenth Century. Faced with the experience of the American wilderness, we sought, in the capacity of pioneers, to find a new basis for culture in the primitive ways of forest and field, in the occupations of hunter, woodman, miner and pastoral nomad: but these occupations, practiced by people who were as much influenced by the idola of utilitarianism as by the deeper effort of the Romantic Movement, did not lead towards a durable culture: the pioneer environment became favorable to an even bleaker preoccupation with the abstractions of matter, money, and political rights. In this situation, the notion of a complete society, carrying on a complete and symmetrical life, tended to disappear from the minds of every one except the disciples of Fourier; with the result that business, technology, and science not merely occupied their legitimate place but took to themselves all that had hitherto belonged to art, religion, and poetry. Positive knowledge and practical action, which are indispensable elements in every culture, became the only living sources of our own; and as the Nineteenth Century wore on, we moved within an ever narrower circle of experience, living mean and illiberal lives.

The moving out of Europe was not merely due to the lure of free land and a multitude of succulent foods: it pointed to cultural vacancy. For three centuries the best minds in Europe had either been trying to get nourishment from the leftovers of classic culture or the Middle Ages, or they had been trying to reach some older source of experience, in order to supplement their bare spiritual fare. Science built up a new conception of the universe, and it endowed its disciples with the power to understand—and frequently to control—external events; but it achieved these results by treating men's central interests and desires as negligible, ignoring the fact that science itself was but a mode of man's activity as a living creature, and that its effort to cancel out the human element was only a very ingenious human expedient. In America, it was easy for an Emerson or a Whitman to see the importance of welding together the interests which science represented, and those which, through the accidents of its historic development, science denied. Turning from a limited European past to a wider heritage, guiding themselves by all the reports of their own day, these poets continued the old voyages of exploration on the plane of the mind, and, seeking passage to India, found themselves coasting along strange shores. None of the fine minds of the Golden Day was afraid to welcome the new forces that were at large in the world. Need I recall that Whitman wrote an apostrophe to the locomotive, that Emerson said a steamship sailing promptly between America and Europe might be as beautiful as a star, and that Thoreau, who loved to hear the wind in the pine needles, listened with equal pleasure to the music of the telegraph wires?

That practical instrumentalities were to be worshiped, never occurred to these writers; but that they added a new and significant element to our culture, which the poet was ready to absorb and include in his report upon the universe, was profoundly true. It is this awareness of new sources of experience that distinguishes the American writers of the Golden Day from their contemporaries in Europe. That the past was merely provisional, and that the future might be formed afresh were two patent generalizations which they drew directly from their environment. These perceptions called, of course, for great works of the imagination; for in proportion as intelligence was dealing more effectually with the instrumentalities of life, it became more necessary for the imagination to project more complete and satisfying ends. The attempt to pre-figure in the imagination a culture which should grow out of and refine the experiences the transplanted European encountered on the new soil, mingling the social heritage of the past with the experience of the present, was the great activity of the Golden Day: the essays of Emerson, the poems of Whitman, the solitary musings of Melville all clustered around this central need. None of these men was caught by the dominant abstractions: each saw life whole, and sought a whole life.

We cannot return to the America of the Golden Day, nor keep it fixed in the postures it once naturally assumed; and we should be far from the spirit of Emerson or Whitman if we attempted to do this. But the principal writers of that time are essential links between our own lives and that earlier, that basic, America. In their work, we can see in pristine state the essential characteristics that still lie under the surface: and from their example, we can more readily find our own foundations, and make our own particular point of departure. In their imaginations, a new world began to form out of the distracting chaos: wealth was in its place, and science was in its place, and the deeper life of man began again to emerge, no longer stunted or frustrated by the instrumentalities it had conceived and set to work. For us who share their vision, a revival of the moribund, or a relapse into the pragmatic acquiescence is equally impossible; and we begin again to dream Thoreau's dream—of what it means to live a whole human life.

A complete culture leads to the nurture of the good life; it permits the fullest use, or sublimation, of man's natural functions and activities. Confronted by the raw materials of existence, a culture works them over into new patterns, in which the woof of reality is crossed by the warp of desire. Love is the type of desire in all its modes; and in the recent emergence of a handful of artists who by the force of their inner life have seen the inessential and makeshift character of a large part of the daily routine, there is perhaps the prophecy of a new stream of tendency in American life.

Henry Adams, in his Education, observed that the American artist, in distinction to all the great writers of classic times, seemed scarcely conscious of the power of sex: he was aware of neither a Virgin nor a Venus. In the works of Sherwood Anderson, Edna Millay, Eugene O'Neill, and Waldo Frank this aversion has disappeared: human passion comes back to the scene with almost volcanic exuberance, drawing all the habits and conventionalities and prudences in its wake. It is through brooding over their sexual experience that Mr. Anderson's characters begin to perceive the weaknesses, the limitations, the sordidness of the life about them: they awaken with the eagerness of a new adolescence to discover, like the father in Many Marriages, that what seemed to them "real life," the externalisms, the business arrangements, the neat routine of office and factory, was in fact an unrelated figment, something which drew upon a boyish self that made sandpiles, whittled sticks, or played soldier and wanted to be captain. Whereas the deep and disruptive force that rouses them, and makes beauty credible and desire realizable, is not, as the Gradgrinds would have it, a dream at all, but the prelude to every enduring reality.

Desire is real! Sherwood Anderson's people come to this, as to a final revelation. But if sexual desire, why not every human desire? In full lust of life man is not merely a poor creature, wryly adjusting himself to external circumstances: he is also a creator, an artist, making circumstances conform to the aims and necessities he himself freely imposes. "Sooner murder an infant in its cradle," wrote William Blake, "than nurse unacted desires"; and in the deep sense of Blake's application, this covers every aspect of life, since a failure of desire, imagination, and vision tends to spread over into every activity. Practical intelligence and a prudent adjustment to externalities are useful only in a secondary position: they are but props to straighten the plant when it begins to grow: at the bottom of it all must be a soil and a seed, an inner burgeoning, an eagerness of life. Art in its many forms is a union of imaginative desire, desire sublimated and socialized, with actuality: without this union, desires become idiotic, and actualities perhaps even a little more so. It is not that our instrumental activities are mean: far from it: but that life is mean when it is entirely absorbed in instrumental activities. Beneath the organized vivacity of our American communities, who is not aware of a blankness, a sterility, a boredom, a despair? Their activity, their very lust, is the galvanic response to an external stimulus, given by an organism that is dead.

The power to escape from this sinister world can come only by the double process of encountering more complete modes of life, and of reformulating a more vital tissue of ideas and symbols to supplant those which have led us into the stereotyped interests and actions which we endeavor in vain to identify with a full human existence. We must rectify the abstract framework of ideas which we have used, in lieu of a full culture, these last few centuries. In part, we shall achieve this by a criticism of the past, which will bring into the foreground those things that have been left out of the current scheme of life and thought. Mr. A. N. Whitehead's Science and the Modern World, and Mr. Victor Branford's Science and Sanctity are landmarks towards this new exploration; for they both suggest the groundwork of a philosophy which shall be oriented as completely towards Life as the dominant thought since Descartes has been directed towards the Machine. To take advantage of our experience and our social heritage and to help in creating this new idolum is not the smallest adventure our generation may know. It is more imaginative than the dreams of the transcendentalist, more practical than the work of the pragmatists, more drastic than the criticisms of the old social revolutionists, and more deeply cultural than all our early attempts to possess the simulacra of culture. It is nothing less than the effort to conceive a new world.

Allons! the road is before us!

CATALOGUE OF DOVER BOOKS

Language Books and Records

GERMAN: HOW TO SPEAK AND WRITE IT. AN INFORMAL CONVERSATIONAL METHOD FOR SELF STUDY, Joseph Rosenberg. Eminently useful for self study because of concentration on elementary stages of learning. Also provides teachers with remarkable variety of aids: 28 full- and double-page sketches with pertinent items numbered and identified in German and English; German proverbs, jokes; grammar, idiom studies; extensive practice exercises. The most interesting introduction to German available, full of amusing illustrations, photographs of cities and landmarks in German-speaking cities, cultural information subtly woven into conversational material. Includes summary of grammar, guide to letter writing, study guide to German literature by Dr. Richard Friedenthal. Index. 400 illustrations. 384pp. 5⅜ x 8½.
T271 Paperbound **$2.00**

FRENCH: HOW TO SPEAK AND WRITE IT. AN INFORMAL CONVERSATIONAL METHOD FOR SELF STUDY, Joseph Lemaitre. Even the absolute beginner can acquire a solid foundation for further study from this delightful elementary course. Photographs, sketches and drawings, sparkling colloquial conversations on a wide variety of topics (including French culture and custom), French sayings and quips, are some of aids used to demonstrate rather than merely describe the language. Thorough yet surprisingly entertaining approach, excellent for teaching and for self study. Comprehensive analysis of pronunciation, practice exercises and appendices of verb tables, additional vocabulary, other useful material. Index. Appendix. 400 illustrations. 416pp. 5⅜ x 8½.
T268 Paperbound **$2.00**

DICTIONARY OF SPOKEN SPANISH, Spanish-English, English-Spanish. Compiled from spoken Spanish, emphasizing idiom and colloquial usage in both Castilian and Latin-American. More than 16,000 entries containing over 25,000 idioms—the largest list of idiomatic constructions ever published. Complete sentences given, indexed under single words—language in immediately useable form, for travellers, businessmen, students, etc. 25 page introduction provides rapid survey of sounds, grammar, syntax, with full consideration of irregular verbs. Especially apt in modern treatment of phrases and structure. 17 page glossary gives translations of geographical names, money values, numbers, national holidays, important street signs, useful expressions of high frequency, plus unique 7 page glossary of Spanish and Spanish-American foods and dishes. Originally published as War Department Technical Manual TM 30-900. iv + 513pp. 5⅜ x 8.
T495 Paperbound **$1.75**

SPEAK MY LANGUAGE: SPANISH FOR YOUNG BEGINNERS, M. Ahlman, Z. Gilbert. Records provide one of the best, and most entertaining, methods of introducing a foreign language to children. Within the framework of a train trip from Portugal to Spain, an English-speaking child is introduced to Spanish by a native companion. (Adapted from a successful radio program of the N. Y. State Educational Department.) Though a continuous story, there are a dozen specific categories of expressions, including greetings, numbers, time, weather, food, clothes, family members, etc. Drill is combined with poetry and contextual use. Authentic background music is heard. An accompanying book enables a reader to follow the records, and includes a vocabulary of over 350 recorded expressions. Two 10″ 33⅓ records, total of 40 minutes. Book. 40 illustrations. 69pp. 5¼ x 10½.
T890 The set **$4.95**

AN ENGLISH-FRENCH-GERMAN-SPANISH WORD FREQUENCY DICTIONARY, H. S. Eaton. An indispensable language study aid, this is a semantic frequency list of the 6000 most frequently used words in 4 languages—24,000 words in all. The lists, based on concepts rather than words alone, and containing all modern, exact, and idiomatic vocabulary, are arranged side by side to form a unique 4-language dictionary. A simple key indicates the importance of the individual words within each language. Over 200 pages of separate indexes for each language enable you to locate individual words at a glance. Will help language teachers and students, authors of textbooks, grammars, and language tests to compare concepts in the various languages and to concentrate on basic vocabulary, avoiding uncommon and obsolete words. 2 Appendixes. xxi + 441pp. 6½ x 9¼.
T738 Paperbound **$2.75**

NEW RUSSIAN-ENGLISH AND ENGLISH-RUSSIAN DICTIONARY, M. A. O'Brien. Over 70,000 entries in the new orthography! Many idiomatic uses and colloquialisms which form the basis of actual speech. Irregular verbs, perfective and imperfective aspects, regular and irregular sound changes, and other features. One of the few dictionaries where accent changes within the conjugation of verbs and the declension of nouns are fully indicated. "One of the best," Prof. E. J. Simmons, Cornell. First names, geographical terms, bibliography, etc. 738pp. 4½ x 6¼.
T208 Paperbound **$2.00**

96 MOST USEFUL PHRASES FOR TOURISTS AND STUDENTS in English, French, Spanish, German, Italian. A handy folder you'll want to carry with you. How to say "Excuse me," "How much is it?", "Write it down, please," etc., in four foreign languages. Copies limited, no more than 1 to a customer.
FREE

Social Sciences

SOCIAL THOUGHT FROM LORE TO SCIENCE, H. E. Barnes and H. Becker. An immense survey of sociological thought and ways of viewing, studying, planning, and reforming society from earliest times to the present. Includes thought on society of preliterate peoples, ancient non-Western cultures, and every great movement in Europe, America, and modern Japan. Analyzes hundreds of great thinkers: Plato, Augustine, Bodin, Vico, Montesquieu, Herder, Comte, Marx, etc. Weighs the contributions of utopians, sophists, fascists and communists: economists, jurists, philosophers, ecclesiastics, and every 19th and 20th century school of scientific sociology, anthropology, and social psychology throughout the world. Combines topical, chronological, and regional approaches, treating the evolution of social thought as a process rather than as a series of mere topics. "Impressive accuracy, competence, and discrimination . . . easily the best single survey," Nation. Thoroughly revised, with new material up to 1960. 2 indexes. Over 2200 bibliographical notes. Three volume set. Total of 1586pp. 5⅜ x 8.

T901 Vol I Paperbound **$2.50**
T902 Vol II Paperbound **$2.50**
T903 Vol III Paperbound **$2.50**
The set **$7.50**

FOLKWAYS, William Graham Sumner. A classic of sociology, a searching and thorough examination of patterns of behaviour from primitive, ancient Greek and Judaic, Medieval Christian, African, Oriental, Melanesian, Australian, Islamic, to modern Western societies. Thousands of illustrations of social, sexual, and religious customs, mores, laws, and institutions. Hundreds of categories: Labor, Wealth, Abortion, Primitive Justice, Life Policy, Slavery, Cannibalism, Uncleanness and the Evil Eye, etc. Will extend the horizon of every reader by showing the relativism of his own culture. Prefatory note by A. G. Keller. Introduction by William Lyon Phelps. Bibliography. Index. xiii + 692pp. 5⅜ x 8.   T508 Paperbound **$2.49**

PRIMITIVE RELIGION, P. Radin. A thorough treatment by a noted anthropologist of the nature and origin of man's belief in the supernatural and the influences that have shaped religious expression in primitive societies. Ranging from the Arunta, Ashanti, Aztec, Bushman, Crow, Fijian, etc., of Africa, Australia, Pacific Islands, the Arctic, North and South America, Prof. Radin integrates modern psychology, comparative religion, and economic thought with first-hand accounts gathered by himself and other scholars of primitive initiations, training of the shaman, and other fascinating topics. "Excellent," NATURE (London). Unabridged reissue of 1st edition. New author's preface. Bibliographic notes. Index. x + 322pp. 5⅜ x 8.
T393 Paperbound **$2.00**

PRIMITIVE MAN AS PHILOSOPHER, P. Radin. A standard anthropological work covering primitive thought on such topics as the purpose of life, marital relations, freedom of thought, symbolism, death, resignation, the nature of reality, personality, gods, and many others. Drawn from factual material gathered from the Winnebago, Oglala Sioux, Maori, Baganda, Batak, Zuni, among others, it does not distort ideas by removing them from context but interprets strictly within the original framework. Extensive selections of original primitive documents. Bibliography. Index. xviii + 402pp. 5⅜ x 8.   T392 Paperbound **$2.25**

A TREATISE ON SOCIOLOGY, THE MIND AND SOCIETY, Vilfredo Pareto. This treatise on human society is one of the great classics of modern sociology. First published in 1916, its careful catalogue of the innumerable manifestations of non-logical human conduct (Book One); the theory of "residues," leading to the premise that sentiment not logic determines human behavior (Book Two), and of "derivations," beliefs derived from desires (Book Three); and the general description of society made up of non-elite and elite, consisting of "foxes" who live by cunning and "lions" who live by force, stirred great controversy. But Pareto's passion for isolation and classification of elements and factors, and his allegiance to scientific method as the key tool for scrutinizing the human situation made his a truly twentieth-century mind and his work a catalytic influence on certain later social commentators. These four volumes (bound as two) require no special training to be appreciated and any reader who wishes to gain a complete understanding of modern sociological theory, regardless of special field of interest, will find them a must. Reprint of revised (corrected) printing of original edition. Translated by Andrew Bongiorno and Arthur Livingston. Index. Bibliography. Appendix containing index-summary of theorems. 48 diagrams. Four volumes bound as two. Total of 2063pp. 5⅜ x 8½.   The set Clothbound **$15.00**

THE POLISH PEASANT IN EUROPE AND AMERICA, William I. Thomas, Florian Znaniecki. A seminal sociological study of peasant primary groups (family and community) and the disruptions produced by a new industrial system and immigration to America. The peasant's family, class system, religious and aesthetic attitudes, and economic life are minutely examined and analyzed in hundreds of pages of primary documentation, particularly letters between family members. The disorientation caused by new environments is scrutinized in detail (a 312-page autobiography of an immigrant is especially valuable and revealing) in an attempt to find common experiences and reactions. The famous "Methodological Note" sets forth the principles which guided the authors. When out of print this set has sold for as much as $50. 2nd revised edition. 2 vols. Vol. 1: xv + 1115pp. Vol. 2: 1135pp. Index. 6 x 9.
T478 Clothbound 2 vol. set **$12.50**

Music

A GENERAL HISTORY OF MUSIC, Charles Burney. A detailed coverage of music from the Greeks up to 1789, with full information on all types of music: sacred and secular, vocal and instrumental, operatic and symphonic. Theory, notation, forms, instruments, innovators, composers, performers, typical and important works, and much more in an easy, entertaining style. Burney covered much of Europe and spoke with hundreds of authorities and composers so that this work is more than a compilation of records . . . it is a living work of careful and first-hand scholarship. Its account of thoroughbass (18th century) Italian music is probably still the best introduction on the subject. A recent NEW YORK TIMES review said, "Surprisingly few of Burney's statements have been invalidated by modern research . . . still of great value." Edited and corrected by Frank Mercer. 35 figures. Indices. 1915pp. 5⅜ x 8. 2 volumes. **T36 The Set, Clothbound $12.50**

A DICTIONARY OF HYMNOLOGY, John Julian. This exhaustive and scholarly work has become known as an invaluable source of hundreds of thousands of important and often difficult to obtain facts on the history and use of hymns in the western world. Everyone interested in hymns will be fascinated by the accounts of famous hymns and hymn writers and amazed by the amount of practical information he will find. More than 30,000 entries on individual hymns, giving authorship, date and circumstances of composition, publication, textual variations, translations, denominational and ritual usage, etc. Biographies of more than 9,000 hymn writers, and essays on important topics such as Christmas carols and children's hymns, and much other unusual and valuable information. A 200 page double-columned index of first lines — the largest in print. Total of 1786 pages in two reinforced clothbound volumes. 6¼ x 9¼. **The set, T333 Clothbound $17.50**

MUSIC IN MEDIEVAL BRITAIN, F. Ll. Harrison. The most thorough, up-to-date, and accurate treatment of the subject ever published, beautifully illustrated. Complete account of institutions and choirs; carols, masses, and motets; liturgy and plainsong; and polyphonic music from the Norman Conquest to the Reformation. Discusses the various schools of music and their reciprocal influences; the origin and development of new ritual forms; development and use of instruments; and new evidence on many problems of the period. Reproductions of scores, over 200 excerpts from medieval melodies. Rules of harmony and dissonance; influence of Continental styles; great composers (Dunstable, Cornysh, Fairfax, etc.); and much more. Register and index of more than 400 musicians. Index of titles. General Index. 225-item bibliography. 6 Appendices. xix + 491pp. 5⅜ x 8¾. **T705 Clothbound $10.00**

THE MUSIC OF SPAIN, Gilbert Chase. Only book in English to give concise, comprehensive account of Iberian music; new Chapter covers music since 1941. Victoria, Albéniz, Cabezón, Pedrell, Turina, hundreds of other composers; popular and folk music; the Gypsies; the guitar; dance, theatre, opera, with only extensive discussion in English of the Zarzuela; virtuosi such as Casals; much more. "Distinguished . . . readable," Saturday Review. 400-item bibliography. Index. 27 photos. 383pp. 5⅜ x 8. **T549 Paperbound $2.25**

ON STUDYING SINGING, Sergius Kagen. An intelligent method of voice-training, which leads you around pitfalls that waste your time, money, and effort. Exposes rigid, mechanical systems, baseless theories, deleterious exercises. "Logical, clear, convincing . . . dead right," Virgil Thomson, N.Y. Herald Tribune. "I recommend this volume highly," Maggie Teyte, Saturday Review. 119pp. 5⅜ x 8. **T622 Paperbound $1.35**

WILLIAM LAWES, M. Lefkowitz. This is the definitive work on Lawes, the versatile, prolific, and highly original "King's musician" of 17th century England. His life is reconstructed from original documents, and nearly every piece he ever wrote is examined and evaluated: his fantasias, pavans, violin "sonatas," lyra viol and bass viol suites, and music for harp and theorbo; and his songs, masques, and theater music to words by Herrick ("Gather Ye Rosebuds"), Jonson, Suckling, Shirley, and others. The author shows the innovations of dissonance, augmented triad, and other Italian influences Lawes helped introduce to England. List of Lawes' complete works and several complete scores by this major precursor of Purcell and the 18th century developments. Index. 5 Appendices. 52 musical excerpts, many never before in print. Bibliography. x + 320pp. 5⅜ x 8. **T706 Clothbound $10.00**

THE FUGUE IN BEETHOVEN'S PIANO MUSIC, J. V. Cockshoot. The first study of a neglected aspect of Beethoven's genius: his ability as a writer of fugues. Analyses of early studies and published works demonstrate his original and powerful contributions to composition. 34 works are examined, with 143 musical excerpts. For all pianists, teachers, students, and music-minded readers with a serious interest in Beethoven. Index. 93-item bibliography. Illustration of original score for "Fugue in C." xv + 212pp. 5⅜ x 8⅜. **T704 Clothbound $6.00**

CATALOGUE OF DOVER BOOKS

JOHANN SEBASTIAN BACH, Philipp Spitta. The complete and unabridged text of the definitive study of Bach. Written some 70 years ago, it is still unsurpassed for its coverage of nearly all aspects of Bach's life and work. There could hardly be a finer non-technical introduction to Bach's music than the detailed, lucid analyses which Spitta provides for hundreds of individual pieces. 26 solid pages are devoted to the B minor mass, for example, and 30 pages to the glorious St. Matthew Passion. This monumental set also includes a major analysis of the music of the 18th century: Buxtehude, Pachelbel, etc. "Unchallenged as the last word on one of the supreme geniuses of music," John Barkham, SATURDAY REVIEW SYNDICATE. Total of 1819pp. 2 volumes. Heavy cloth binding. 5⅜ x 8. T252 The set, Clothbound **$13.50**

THE LIFE OF MOZART, O. Jahn. Probably the largest amount of material on Mozart's life and works ever gathered together in one book! Its 1350 authoritative and readable pages cover every event in his life, and contain a full critique of almost every piece he ever wrote, including sketches and intimate works. There is a full historical-cultural background, and vast research into musical and literary history, sources of librettos, prior treatments of Don Juan legend, etc. This is the complete and unaltered text of the definitive Townsend translation, with foreword by Grove. 5 engraved portraits from Salzburg archives. 4 facsimiles in Mozart's hand. 226 musical examples. 4 Appendixes, including complete list of Mozart's compositions, with Köchel numbers (fragmentary works included). Total of xxviii + 1352pp. Three volume set. 5⅜ x 8.

T85 Vol. I Clothbound **$5.00**
T86 Vol. II Clothbound **$5.00**
The set **$10.00**

BEETHOVEN'S QUARTETS, J. de Marliave. The most complete and authoritative study ever written, enjoyable for scholar and layman alike. The 16 quartets and Grand Fugue are all analyzed bar by bar and theme by theme, not over-technically, but concentrating on mood and effects. Complete background material for each composition: influences, first reviews, etc. Preface by Gabriel Fauré. Introduction and notes by J. Escarra. Translated by Hilda Andrews. 321 musical examples. xxiii + 379pp. 5⅜ x 8. T694 Paperbound **$2.00**

STRUCTURAL HEARING: TONAL COHERENCE IN MUSIC, Felix Salzer. Written by a pupil of the late Heinrich Schenker, this is not only the most thorough exposition in English of the Schenker method but also extends the Schenker approach to include modern music, the middle ages, and renaissance music. It explores the phenomenon of tonal organization by means of a detailed analysis and discussion of more than 500 musical pieces. It casts new light for the reader acquainted with harmony upon the understanding of musical compositions, problems of musical coherence, and connection between theory and composition. "Has been the foundation on which all teaching in music theory has been based at this college," Leopold Mannes, President of The Mannes College of Music. 2 volumes. Total of 658pp. 6½ x 9¼. The set, T418 Clothbound **$8.00**

ANTONIO STRADIVARI: HIS LIFE AND WORK (1644-1737), W. Henry Hill, Arthur F. Hill, and Alfred E. Hill. Still the only book that really delves into life and art of the incomparable Italian craftsman, maker of the finest musical instruments in the world today. The authors, expert violin-makers themselves, discuss Stradivari's ancestry, his construction and finishing techniques, distinguished characteristics of many of his instruments and their locations. Included, too, is story of introduction of his instruments into France, England, first revelation of their supreme merit, and information on his labels, number of instruments made, prices, mystery of ingredients of his varnish, tone of pre-1684 Stradivari violin and changes between 1684 and 1690. An extremely interesting, informative account for all music lovers, from craftsman to concert-goer. Republication of original (1902) edition. New introduction by Sydney Beck, Head of Rare Book and Manuscript Collections, Music Division, New York Public Library. Analytical index by Rembert Wurlitzer. Appendixes. 68 illustrations. 30 full-page plates. 4 in color. xxvi + 315pp. 5⅜ x 8½. T425 Paperbound **$2.25**

THREE CLASSICS IN THE AESTHETIC OF MUSIC, Claude Debussy, Ferrucio Busoni, and Charles Ives. Three very different points of view by three top-ranking modern composers. "M. Croche, the Dilettante-Hater" consists of twenty-five brief articles written by Debussy between the years 1901 and 1905, a sparkling collection of personal commentary on a wide range of topics. Busoni's "Toward a New Aesthetic of Music" considers the nature of absolute music in an attempt to suggest answers to the question, What are the aims of music?, and discusses modern systems of tonality and harmony, the concept of unity of keys, etc. Ives's "Essays Before a Sonata," a literary complement to the movements of the author's "Concord, 1845" piano sonata, contains his most mature analysis of his art. Stimulating reading for musicians, music lovers, and philosophers of the arts. iv + 188pp. 5⅜ x 8½. T320 Paperbound **$1.50**

Philosophy, Religion

GUIDE TO PHILOSOPHY, C. E. M. Joad. A modern classic which examines many crucial problems which man has pondered through the ages: Does free will exist? Is there plan in the universe? How do we know and validate our knowledge? Such opposed solutions as subjective idealism and realism, chance and teleology, vitalism and logical positivism, are evaluated and the contributions of the great philosophers from the Greeks to moderns like Russell, Whitehead, and others, are considered in the context of each problem. "The finest introduction," BOSTON TRANSCRIPT. Index. Classified bibliography. 592pp. 5⅜ x 8.
T297 Paperbound **$2.25**

HISTORY OF ANCIENT PHILOSOPHY, W. Windelband. One of the clearest, most accurate comprehensive surveys of Greek and Roman philosophy. Discusses ancient philosophy in general, intellectual life in Greece in the 7th and 6th centuries B.C., Thales, Anaximander, Anaximenes, Heraclitus, the Eleatics, Empedocles, Anaxagoras, Leucippus, the Pythagoreans, the Sophists, Socrates, Democritus (20 pages), Plato (50 pages), Aristotle (70 pages), the Peripatetics, Stoics, Epicureans, Sceptics, Neo-platonists, Christian Apologists, etc. 2nd German edition translated by H. E. Cushman. xv + 393pp. 5⅜ x 8.
T357 Paperbound **$1.85**

ILLUSTRATIONS OF THE HISTORY OF MEDIEVAL THOUGHT AND LEARNING, R. L. Poole. Basic analysis of the thought and lives of the leading philosophers and ecclesiastics from the 8th to the 14th century—Abailard, Ockham, Wycliffe, Marsiglio of Padua, and many other great thinkers who carried the torch of Western culture and learning through the "Dark Ages": political, religious, and metaphysical views. Long a standard work for scholars and one of the best introductions to medieval thought for beginners. Index. 10 Appendices. xiii + 327pp. 5⅜ x 8.
T674 Paperbound **$2.00**

PHILOSOPHY AND CIVILIZATION IN THE MIDDLE AGES, M. de Wulf. This semi-popular survey covers aspects of medieval intellectual life such as religion, philosophy, science, the arts, etc. It also covers feudalism vs. Catholicism, rise of the universities, mendicant orders, monastic centers, and similar topics. Unabridged. Bibliography. Index. viii + 320pp. 5⅜ x 8.
T284 Paperbound **$1.85**

AN INTRODUCTION TO SCHOLASTIC PHILOSOPHY, Prof. M. de Wulf. Formerly entitled SCHOLASTICISM OLD AND NEW, this volume examines the central scholastic tradition from St. Anselm, Albertus Magnus, Thomas Aquinas, up to Suarez in the 17th century. The relation of scholasticism to ancient and medieval philosophy and science in general is clear and easily followed. The second part of the book considers the modern revival of scholasticism, the Louvain position, relations with Kantianism and Positivism. Unabridged. xvi + 271pp. 5⅜ x 8.
T296 Clothbound **$3.50**
T283 Paperbound **$2.00**

A HISTORY OF MODERN PHILOSOPHY, H. Höffding. An exceptionally clear and detailed coverage of western philosophy from the Renaissance to the end of the 19th century. Major and minor men such as Pomponazzi, Bodin, Boehme, Telesius, Bruno, Copernicus, da Vinci, Kepler, Galileo, Bacon, Descartes, Hobbes, Spinoza, Leibniz, Wolff, Locke, Newton, Berkeley, Hume, Erasmus, Montesquieu, Voltaire, Diderot, Rousseau, Lessing, Kant, Herder, Fichte, Schelling, Hegel, Schopenhauer, Comte, Mill, Darwin, Spencer, Hartmann, Lange, and many others, are discussed in terms of theory of knowledge, logic, cosmology, and psychology. Index. 2 volumes, total of 1159pp. 5⅜ x 8.
T117 Vol. 1, Paperbound **$2.50**
T118 Vol. 2, Paperbound **$2.25**

ARISTOTLE, A. E. Taylor. A brilliant, searching non-technical account of Aristotle and his thought written by a foremost Platonist. It covers the life and works of Aristotle; classification of the sciences; logic; first philosophy; matter and form; causes; motion and eternity; God; physics; metaphysics; and similar topics. Bibliography. New Index compiled for this edition. 128pp. 5⅜ x 8.
T280 Paperbound **$1.00**

THE SYSTEM OF THOMAS AQUINAS, M. de Wulf. Leading Neo-Thomist, one of founders of University of Louvain, gives concise exposition to central doctrines of Aquinas, as a means toward determining his value to modern philosophy, religion. Formerly "Medieval Philosophy Illustrated from the System of Thomas Aquinas." Trans. by E. Messenger. Introduction. 151pp. 5⅜ x 8.
T568 Paperbound **$1.25**

LEIBNIZ, H. W. Carr. Most stimulating middle-level coverage of basic philosophical thought of Leibniz. Easily understood discussion, analysis of major works: "Theodicy," "Principles of Nature and Grace," "Monadology"; Leibniz's influence; intellectual growth; correspondence; disputes with Bayle, Malebranche, Newton; importance of his thought today, with reinterpretation in modern terminology. "Power and mastery," London Times. Bibliography. Index. 226pp. 5⅜ x 8.
T624 Paperbound **$1.35**

CATALOGUE OF DOVER BOOKS

AN ESSAY CONCERNING HUMAN UNDERSTANDING, John Locke. Edited by A. C. Fraser. Unabridged reprinting of definitive edition; only complete edition of "Essay" in print. Marginal analyses of almost every paragraph; hundreds of footnotes; authoritative 140-page biographical, critical, historical prolegomena. Indexes. 1170pp. 5⅜ x 8.

T530 Vol. 1 (Books 1, 2) Paperbound **$2.50**
T531 Vol. 2 (Books 3, 4) Paperbound **$2.50**
2 volume set **$5.00**

THE PHILOSOPHY OF HISTORY, G. W. F. Hegel. One of the great classics of western thought which reveals Hegel's basic principle: that history is not chance but a rational process, the realization of the Spirit of Freedom. Ranges from the oriental cultures of subjective thought to the classical subjective cultures, to the modern absolute synthesis where spiritual and secular may be reconciled. Translation and introduction by J. Sibree. Introduction by C. Hegel. Special introduction for this edition by Prof. Carl Friedrich. xxxix + 447pp. 5⅜ x 8.

T112 Paperbound **$2.25**

THE PHILOSOPHY OF HEGEL, W. T. Stace. The first detailed analysis of Hegel's thought in English, this is especially valuable since so many of Hegel's works are out of print. Dr. Stace examines Hegel's debt to Greek idealists and the 18th century and then proceeds to a careful description and analysis of Hegel's first principles, categories, reason, dialectic method, his logic, philosophy of nature and spirit, etc. Index. Special 14 x 20 chart of Hegelian system. x + 526pp. 5⅜ x 8.

T254 Paperbound **$2.75**

THE WILL TO BELIEVE and HUMAN IMMORTALITY, W. James. Two complete books bound as one. THE WILL TO BELIEVE discusses the interrelations of belief, will, and intellect in man; chance vs. determinism, free will vs. determinism, free will vs. fate, pluralism vs. monism; the philosophies of Hegel and Spencer, and more. HUMAN IMMORTALITY examines the question of survival after death and develops an unusual and powerful argument for immortality. Two prefaces. Index. Total of 429pp. 5⅜ x 8.

T291 Paperbound **$2.00**

THE WORLD AND THE INDIVIDUAL, Josiah Royce. Only major effort by an American philosopher to interpret nature of things in systematic, comprehensive manner. Royce's formulation of an absolute voluntarism remains one of the original and profound solutions to the problems involved. Part One, Four Historical Conceptions of Being, inquires into first principles, true meaning and place of individuality. Part Two, Nature, Man, and the Moral Order, is application of first principles to problems concerning religion, evil, moral order. Introduction by J. E. Smith, Yale Univ. Index. 1070pp. 5⅜ x 8.

T561 Vol. 1 Paperbound **$2.75**
T562 Vol. 2 Paperbound **$2.75**
Two volume set **$5.50**

THE PHILOSOPHICAL WRITINGS OF PEIRCE, edited by J. Buchler. This book (formerly THE PHILOSOPHY OF PEIRCE) is a carefully integrated exposition of Peirce's complete system composed of selections from his own work. Symbolic logic, scientific method, theory of signs, pragmatism, epistemology, chance, cosmology, ethics, and many other topics are treated by one of the greatest philosophers of modern times. This is the only inexpensive compilation of his key ideas. xvi + 386pp. 5⅜ x 8.

T217 Paperbound **$2.00**

EXPERIENCE AND NATURE, John Dewey. An enlarged, revised edition of the Paul Carus lectures which Dewey delivered in 1925. It covers Dewey's basic formulation of the problem of knowledge, with a full discussion of other systems, and a detailing of his own concepts of the relationship of external world, mind, and knowledge. Starts with a thorough examination of the philosophical method; examines the interrelationship of experience and nature; analyzes experience on basis of empirical naturalism, the formulation of law, role of language and social factors in knowledge; etc. Dewey's treatment of central problems in philosophy is profound but extremely easy to follow. ix + 448pp. 5⅜ x 8.

T471 Paperbound **$2.00**

THE PHILOSOPHICAL WORKS OF DESCARTES. The definitive English edition of all the major philosophical works and letters of René Descartes. All of his revolutionary insights, from his famous "Cogito ergo sum" to his detailed account of contemporary science and his astonishingly fruitful concept that all phenomena of the universe (except mind) could be reduced to clear laws by the use of mathematics. An excellent source for the thought of men like Hobbes, Arnauld, Gassendi, etc., who were Descarte's contemporaries. Translated by E. S. Haldane and G. Ross. Introductory notes. Index. Total of 842pp. 5⅜ x 8.

T71 Vol. 1, Paperbound **$2.00**
T72 Vol. 2, Paperbound **$2.00**

THE CHIEF WORKS OF SPINOZA. An unabridged reprint of the famous Bohn edition containing all of Spinoza's most important works: Vol. I: The Theologico-Political Treatise and the Political Treatise. Vol. II: On The Improvement Of Understanding, The Ethics, Selected Letters. Profound and enduring ideas on God, the universe, pantheism, society, religion, the state, democracy, the mind, emotions, freedom and the nature of man, which influenced Goethe, Hegel, Schelling, Coleridge, Whitehead, and many others. Introduction. 2 volumes. 826pp. 5⅜ x 8.

T249 Vol. I, Paperbound **$1.75**
T250 Vol. II, Paperbound **$1.50**

CATALOGUE OF DOVER BOOKS

THE ANALYSIS OF MATTER, Bertrand Russell. A classic which has retained its importance in understanding the relation between modern physical theory and human perception. Logical analysis of physics, prerelativity physics, causality, scientific inference, Weyl's theory, tensors, invariants and physical interpretations, periodicity, and much more is treated with Russell's usual brilliance. "Masterly piece of clear thinking and clear writing," NATION AND ATHENAE-UM. "Most thorough treatment of the subject," THE NATION. Introduction. Index. 8 figures. viii + 408pp. 5⅜ x 8. S231 Paperbound **$1.95**

CONCEPTUAL THINKING (A LOGICAL INQUIRY), S. Körner. Discusses origin, use of general concepts on which language is based, and the light they shed on basic philosophical questions. Rigorously examines how different concepts are related; how they are linked to experience; problems in the field of contact between exact logical, mathematical, and scientific concepts, and the inexactness of everyday experience (studied at length). This work elaborates many new approaches to the traditional problems of philosophy—epistemology, value theories, metaphysics, aesthetics, morality. "Rare originality . . . brings a new rigour into philosophical argument," Philosophical Quarterly. New corrected second edition. Index. vii + 301pp. 5⅜ x 8. T516 Paperbound **$1.75**

INTRODUCTION TO SYMBOLIC LOGIC, S. Langer. No special knowledge of math required — probably the clearest book ever written on symbolic logic, suitable for the layman, general scientist, and philosopher. You start with simple symbols and advance to a knowledge of the Boole-Schroeder and Russell-Whitehead systems. Forms, logical structure, classes, the calculus of propositions, logic of the syllogism, etc., are all covered. "One of the clearest and simplest introductions," MATHEMATICS GAZETTE. Second enlarged, revised edition. 368pp. 5⅜ x 8. S164 Paperbound **$1.85**

LANGUAGE, TRUTH AND LOGIC, A. J. Ayer. A clear, careful analysis of the basic ideas of Logical Positivism. Building on the work of Schlick, Russell, Carnap, and the Viennese School, Mr. Ayer develops a detailed exposition of the nature of philosophy, science, and metaphysics; the Self and the World; logic and common sense, and other philosophic concepts. An aid to clarity of thought as well as the first full-length development of Logical Positivism in English. Introduction by Bertrand Russell. Index. 160pp. 5⅜ x 8. T10 Paperbound **$1.25**

ESSAYS IN EXPERIMENTAL LOGIC, J. Dewey. Based upon the theory that knowledge implies a judgment which in turn implies an inquiry, these papers consider the inquiry stage in terms of: the relationship of thought and subject matter, antecedents of thought, data and meanings. 3 papers examine Bertrand Russell's thought, while 2 others discuss pragmatism and a final essay presents a new theory of the logic of values. Index. viii + 444pp. 5⅜ x 8. T73 Paperbound **$2.25**

TRAGIC SENSE OF LIFE, M. de Unamuno. The acknowledged masterpiece of one of Spain's most influential thinkers. Between the despair at the inevitable death of man and all his works and the desire for something better, Unamuno finds that "saving incertitude" that alone can console us. This dynamic appraisal of man's faith in God and in himself has been called "a masterpiece" by the ENCYCLOPAEDIA BRITANNICA. xxx + 332pp. 5⅜ x 8. T257 Paperbound **$2.00**

HISTORY OF DOGMA, A. Harnack. Adolph Harnack, who died in 1930, was perhaps the greatest Church historian of all time. In this epoch-making history, which has never been surpassed in comprehensiveness and wealth of learning, he traces the development of the authoritative Christian doctrinal system from its first crystallization in the 4th century down through the Reformation, including also a brief survey of the later developments through the Infallibility decree of 1870. He reveals the enormous influence of Greek thought on the early Fathers, and discusses such topics as the Apologists, the great councils, Manichaeism, the historical position of Augustine, the medieval opposition to indulgences, the rise of Protestantism, the relations of Luther's doctrines with modern tendencies of thought, and much more. "Monumental work; still the most valuable history of dogma . . . luminous analysis of the problems . . . abounds in suggestion and stimulus and can be neglected by no one who desires to understand the history of thought in this most important field," Dutcher's Guide to Historical Literature. Translated by Neil Buchanan. Index. Unabridged reprint in 4 volumes. Vol I: Beginnings to the Gnostics and Marcion. Vol II & III: 2nd century to the 4th century Fathers. Vol IV & V: 4th century Councils to the Carlovingian Renaissance. Vol VI & VII: Period of Clugny (c. 1000) to the Reformation, and after. Total of cii + 2407pp. 5⅜ x 8.

T904 Vol I	Paperbound	**$2.50**
T905 Vol II & III	Paperbound	**$2.75**
T906 Vol IV & V	Paperbound	**$2.75**
T907 Vol VI & VII	Paperbound	**$2.75**
	The set	**$10.75**

THE GUIDE FOR THE PERPLEXED, Maimonides. One of the great philosophical works of all time and a necessity for everyone interested in the philosophy of the Middle Ages in the Jewish, Christian, and Moslem traditions. Maimonides develops a common meeting-point for the Old Testament and the Aristotelian thought which pervaded the medieval world. His ideas and methods predate such scholastics as Aquinas and Scotus and throw light on the entire problem of philosophy or science vs. religion. 2nd revised edition. Complete unabridged Friedländer translation. 55 page introduction to Maimonides's life, period, etc., with an important summary of the GUIDE. Index. lix + 414pp. 5⅜ x 8. T351 Paperbound **$2.00**

History, Political Science

THE POLITICAL THOUGHT OF PLATO AND ARISTOTLE, E. Barker. One of the clearest and most accurate expositions of the corpus of Greek political thought. This standard source contains exhaustive analyses of the "Republic" and other Platonic dialogues and Aristotle's "Politics" and "Ethics," and discusses the origin of these ideas in Greece, contributions of other Greek theorists, and modifications of Greek ideas by thinkers from Aquinas to Hegel. "Must" reading for anyone interested in the history of Western thought. Index. Chronological Table of Events. 2 Appendixes. xxiv + 560pp. 5⅜ x 8. **T521 Paperbound $2.50**

THE IDEA OF PROGRESS, J. B. Bury. Practically unknown before the Reformation, the idea of progress has since become one of the central concepts of western civilization. Prof. Bury analyzes its evolution in the thought of Greece, Rome, the Middle Ages, the Renaissance, to its flowering in all branches of science, religion, philosophy, industry, art, and literature, during and following the 16th century. Introduction by Charles Beard. Index. xl + 357pp. 5⅜ x 8. **T40 Paperbound $1.95**

THE ANCIENT GREEK HISTORIANS, J. B. Bury. This well known, easily read work covers the entire field of classical historians from the early writers to Herodotus, Thucydides, Xenophon, through Poseidonius and such Romans as Tacitus, Cato, Caesar, Livy. Scores of writers are studied biographically, in style, sources, accuracy, structure, historical concepts, and influences. Recent discoveries such as the Oxyrhinchus papyri are referred to, as well as such great scholars as Nissen, Gomperz, Cornford, etc. "Totally unblemished by pedantry." Outlook. "The best account in English," Dutcher, A Guide to Historical Lit. Bibliography, Index. x + 281pp. 5⅜ x 8. **T397 Paperbound $1.65**

HISTORY OF THE LATER ROMAN EMPIRE, J. B. Bury. This standard work by the leading Byzantine scholar of our time discusses the later Roman and early Byzantine empires from 395 A.D. through the death of Justinian in 565, in their political, social, cultural, theological, and military aspects. Contemporary documents are quoted in full, making this the most complete reconstruction of the period and a fit successor to Gibbon's "Decline and Fall." "Most unlikely that it will ever be superseded," Glanville Downey, Dumbarton Oaks Research Lib. Geneological tables. 5 maps. Bibliography. Index. 2 volumes total of 965pp. 5⅜ x 8. **T398, 399 Two volume set, Paperbound $4.50**

A HISTORY OF ANCIENT GEOGRAPHY, E. H. Bunbury. Standard study, in English, of ancient geography; never equalled for scope, detail. First full account of history of geography from Greeks' first world picture based on mariners, through Ptolemy. Discusses every important map, discovery, figure, travel expedition, war, conjecture, narrative, bearing on subject. Chapters on Homeric geography, Herodotus, Alexander expedition, Strabo, Pliny, Ptolemy, would stand alone as exhaustive monographs. Includes minor geographers, men not usually regarded in this context: Hecataeus, Pytheas, Hipparchus, Artemidorus, Marinus of Tyre, etc. Uses information gleaned from military campaigns such as Punic Wars, Hannibal's passage of Alps, campaigns of Lucullus, Pompey, Caesar's wars, the Trojan War. New introduction by W. H. Stahl, Brooklyn College. Bibliography. Index. 20 maps. 1426pp. 5⅜ x 8. **T570-1, clothbound, 2-volume set $12.50**

POLITICAL PARTIES, Robert Michels. Classic of social science, reference point for all later work, deals with nature of leadership in social organization on government and trade union levels. Probing tendency of oligarchy to replace democracy, it studies need for leadership, desire for organization, psychological motivations, vested interests, hero worship, reaction of leaders to power, press relations, many other aspects. Trans. by E. & C. Paul. Introduction. 447pp. 5⅜ x 8. **T569 Paperbound $2.00**

A HISTORY OF HISTORICAL WRITING, Harry Elmer Barnes. Virtually the only adequate survey of the whole course of historical writing in a single volume. Surveys developments from the beginnings of historiographies in the ancient Near East and the Classical World, up through the Cold War. Covers major historians in detail, shows interrelationship with cultural background, makes clear individual contributions, evaluates and estimates importance; also enormously rich upon minor authors and thinkers who are usually passed over. Packed with scholarship and learning, clear, easily written. Indispensable to every student of history. Revised and enlarged up to 1961. Index and bibliography. xv + 442pp. 5⅜ x 8½. **T104 Paperbound $2.25**

Prices subject to change without notice.

Dover publishes books on art, music, philosophy, literature, languages, history, social sciences, psychology, handcrafts, orientalia, puzzles and entertainments, chess, pets and gardens, books explaining science, intermediate and higher mathematics, mathematical physics, engineering, biological sciences, earth sciences, classics of science, etc. Write to:

Dept. catrr.
Dover Publications, Inc.
180 Varick Street, N.Y. 14, N.Y.